REDEFINING
family
WEALTH

REDEFINING
family
WEALTH

A Parent's Guide to Purposeful Living

DEBORAH L. MEYER, CPA/PFS, CFP®

For my boys.
You make my days brighter and life sweeter.

Copyright © 2019 by Deborah Meyer

All rights reserved. No part of this publication may be reproduced, distributed, or transmitted in any form or by any means, including photocopying, recording, or other electronic or mechanical methods, without the prior written permission of the publisher, except in the case of brief quotations embodied in critical reviews and certain other noncommercial uses permitted by copyright law.

For permission requests, write to the publisher, addressed "Attention: Permissions Coordinator," at the address below.

Chasing Grace Press
P.O. Box 1278
St. Charles, MO 63302

ISBN: (print): 978-1-7337926-0-8
ISBN: (ebook): 978-1-7337926-1-5

Ordering Information:
Special discounts are available on quantity purchases by corporations, associations, and others. For details, contact Chasing Grace Press at the address above.

Table of Contents

Introduction ix

Chapter One You Were Made For More 1

Chapter Two Your Past Isn't a Script for Your Future 11

Chapter Three Lead with Values 27

Chapter Four Budget Isn't a Dirty Word 41

Chapter Five
Prepare for Opportunities, Not Just Emergencies 55

Chapter Six Not All Debt is Evil 67

Chapter Seven
Value-Based Investing Works 83

Chapter Eight Even the Faithful Have Insurance 97

Chapter Nine
Traditional Retirement Isn't the Answer 115

Chapter Ten Go for Broke 129

Chapter Eleven
Get Your Affairs in Order 141

Chapter Twelve
Cash Won't Pay for College 153

Chapter Thirteen
DIY is Good, but Advisors Are Better 165

Chapter Fourteen
Ready, Set, Go 175

Acknowledgments 181

Notes 183

Introduction

I first read *Money* magazine in middle school and was immediately hooked. At the time, algebra and geometry both seemed so abstract. I wondered how classroom lessons would ever apply to real life, but *Money* opened my eyes to another world, one focused on prudent saving habits and a pathway to building real financial wealth. Furthermore, the magazine was my constant in a constantly changing world.

I grew up predominantly in the Midwest. We moved several times when I was young. And no, my parents weren't in the military. My dad was in the manufacturing industry and felt he had to relocate our family to financially support us whenever one of his employers closed up shop. New city, new friends, new everything.

Things eventually stabilized, and I spent fourth grade through senior year of high school in Wisconsin. Dealing with my dad's unemployment in the seventh and eighth grades was one of my most difficult childhood experiences. Luckily, mom's consistent employment as a CPA helped us keep food on the table and provided stability during crucial times.

I learned about saving money from my part-time job. My parents' hard work ethic and frugality also fostered excellent financial habits in me. When it was time to choose a major in college at Saint Louis University, I decided on accounting. It was nice to follow in the footsteps of my mother, who was such a positive role model.

Over the years, I've realized there are a lot of misconceptions about wealth—especially among Christians. Have you ever heard one of the following statements?

- You can't change. Your financial mistakes will follow you forever.
- Budgets are restrictive and take the fun out of life.
- Build an emergency fund equal to three to 12 months of living expenses.
- Debt (and money) is intrinsically evil.
- Investing with your values isn't possible.
- Insurance takes all your financial worries away.
- Retirement at age 65 is the only option.
- Estate planning is reserved for the rich.
- You only need to look out for yourself.
- Don't worry about saving for college. You'll have plenty of cash to pay for it.
- Financial advisors are helpful only if you have at least a million dollars.

All of these are lies. They are stumbling blocks, preventing you from reaching your financial goals. This book will transform the way you think about wealth. I'll turn each of those myths upside down and offer an alternative.

Are you ready to live abundantly? Are you willing to toss out preconceived notions of wealth and boldly move into unchartered territory?

Introduction

We are all shaped by our money behaviors, attitudes, and history. I'm going to challenge you throughout this book to dig deep and uncover your core vision, values, and goals surrounding wealth.

What makes me qualified to speak intelligently about wealth? Let me tell you.

Deloitte, a Big Four public accounting firm, hired me straight out of college. I was fortunate to work with bright, ambitious tax professionals whose technical expertise far surpassed my own. When several of my mentors left Deloitte in 2006, I started looking outside public accounting and landed in a client-facing wealth management role. The next seven years went by quickly. My investment advisory firm's team more than doubled, and our managed assets more than tripled to three billion dollars. That exponential growth prompted leaders of the firm to share a fresh company vision, and they raised the minimum new client fee to $25,000 annually.

That transition was a hard pill for me to swallow. The higher minimum fee meant we were only serving very affluent families, many of whom were already retired. As a Christian, I felt called to help people like me who were both accumulating and sharing wealth. Additionally, some of the charitable causes my clients supported contradicted my pro-life values. It was emotionally difficult to process donation requests on their behalf.

Those seven years also brought about personal change. I married Bryan and we were blessed with two baby boys. Shortly after our second son's birth, I found myself exhausted and drained. Bryan worked full time in a demanding position while attending a rigorous evening MBA program. My daily commute was one and a half hours round-trip. I barely had enough time at night to feed the boys, bathe them, and get ready for bedtime…not to mention the inevitable sleepless nights with a newborn. The pace of our life was unsustainable. Moments that should have been joyful, such as birthday parties and family dinners, felt burdensome instead. My to-do list never seemed to end.

My last day at the wealth management firm was Halloween 2013. Leaving my relationships with coworkers and clients and abandoning a steady paycheck was difficult. But I felt called to do it, and that single decision put my life on a different trajectory.

Fast forward to today. The youngest of our three sons is four years old. In 2016, I launched WorthyNest®, an independent wealth management firm that helps parents build wealth in a way that aligns with their values.

WorthyNest® and Redefining *Family* Wealth are labors of love. "Faith. Family. Finance." is my firm's tagline but it embodies much more. I started writing professionally in 2016, and have been blessed with being able to regularly contribute to Kiplinger's Building Wealth Channel.

This book is a how-to guide for achieving success in a way that aligns with your values. The lessons will resonate most with Christians, but you don't have to be religious to benefit from the messages in this book. The first half of the book focuses on individual reflection and actions you can take to build wealth, while the second half details choices you make that significantly impact others. I hope you enjoy it!

Chapter One

You Were Made For More

You were made for more. We were created out of nothing, and there is a special plan for each of us to live our full potential. Although the path isn't always clear, it's our duty to observe and listen intently. We must open our eyes to the possibilities and tune out distractions. We are called to live purposefully and intentionally.

Wealth isn't just about money. Merriam-Webster defines wealth as the abundance of valuable material possessions or resources, and this definition closely aligns with society's definition of wealth. But what traditional culture defines as wealth directly opposes Christian teaching. We are called to love others. How can we do that if we are solely concerned with accumulating monetary wealth? Spiritual bankruptcy is our biggest challenge.

Common synonyms for wealth are abundance, affluence, capital, riches, security, and treasure. Let's focus on one of these synonyms in particular, capital. According to *Forum for the Future*, there are five types of capital: natural, human, social, manufacturing, and financial.

Capital

Natural capital refers to resources and processes that produce goods and services. For example, you need photos, special glue or tape, accessories such as card stock and ribbons, and an actual book to make a scrapbook. These items represent natural capital.

Human capital includes your health, knowledge, skills, and motivation. You can enhance human capital through education and training. If you are in a highly specialized occupation, you inherently have more human capital than people in blue collar positions. Thus, doctors and attorneys have more human capital than waitresses or cab drivers because they undergo rigorous training and meet certification standards.

From a personal standpoint, I'm a lifelong learner. My undergraduate degree is accounting, but I also prepared for the Certified Financial Planner™ and Certified Public Accountant exams after college. There are continuing education requirements and ethical standards for both CFP® professionals and CPAs. Outside of these continuing education standards, I attend conferences and regularly read. Staying fresh with changes in my industry keeps me motivated. All of these actions enhance my human capital.

Social capital pertains to the institutions and relationships that help human capital flourish. Examples of social institutions include schools, universities, churches, professional associations, and neighborhoods. Saint Louis University helped me grow not only as a student but also as a person. It was the right environment for me to succeed in college and later in life. Church keeps me spiritually focused. Professional organizations such as XY Planning Network,

NAPFA, and FinCon enable me to reach my business potential. Charities offer a tangible way to give back.

Fixed assets and material goods are the foundation of manufactured capital, which is focused on process not output. If you manufacture any type of good—shoes, food, or clothes—your business is heavily dependent on fixed asset machinery and a large space for manufacturing. This type of capital isn't relevant to most people.

Financial capital enables other forms of capital to be owned and traded but holds no intrinsic value. When you think of money, you think of value. But dollars and cents are really just a means of exchange. The bill you hold in your hand does not actually have intrinsic value. The bill is handed to a cashier, who will give you another good in exchange for that money.

> Dollars and cents are really just a means of exchange. The bill you hold in your hand does not actually have intrinsic value.

Too often, we equate wealth with financial capital. It is only one piece of the puzzle. Are you developing human and social capital to the best of your ability? If you are a small business owner, do you use natural and manufactured capital for the greater good?

You are wealthy when living the life God calls you to live. Faith helps you move past fear, courageously into the future. Your relationships with others are strong and solid. You become a supportive parent, sibling, and friend. Your vocation is clear, and you are using your unique talents to serve others. You generously give time to meaningful causes, and you become a wise steward of the financial resources entrusted to you.

Stewardship

Biblical stewardship[1] is where the concepts of faith, work, and economics intersect. The Institute for Faith, Work & Economics defines four principles of stewardship:

- Ownership
- Responsibility
- Accountability
- Reward

Christians know that God owns everything, and we are simply administrators acting on His behalf. We don't actually "own" anything. Greed challenges this assumption on a daily basis.

Furthermore, we must be responsible with how we manage the resources entrusted to us. That responsibility can start now. Even if you have been irresponsible with finances in the past, do not fret. Humans are flawed. That's the beauty of forgiveness and healing.

Accountability is closely tied to responsibility but is slightly different. Responsibility refers to our day-to-day actions, but accountability is more closely tied to our Judgment Day. According to the Institute for Faith, Work &

Economics, we will eventually be "called to give an account of how we have administered everything we have been given, including our time, money, abilities, information, wisdom, relationships, and authority."

If you follow the principles of biblical stewardship, your reward will be in heaven. Matthew Kelly[2] aptly states, "It is God who does the transforming but only to the extent that we cooperate." Your mindset has incredible power over your actions. You must be open and willing to pursue a path less-traveled.

The Importance of Faith

While we are talking about stewardship, let's discuss a related concept…faith.

When is the last time you let fear rule a decision?

Was it this morning? Yesterday? A week ago? A month ago?

Merriam-Webster defines faith as "belief and trust in and loyalty to God." It also offers an alternate definition: "firm belief in something for which there is no proof."

It is easy to think about faith through the lens of the first definition. You either trust in God or you don't. But the alternate definition offers a different perspective on faith. Michael Kitces interviewed Diane MacPhee on the Financial Advisor Success Podcast[3], and Diane shared this related Native American fable:

"One evening, an elder Cherokee told his grandson about a battle that goes on inside all people. He said, 'My son, the battle is between two wolves inside us. One is fear. It carries anxiety, concern, uncertainty, hesitancy, indecision, and inaction. The other is faith. It brings calm, conviction, confidence, enthusiasm, decisiveness, excitement, and action.'

The grandson thought about it for a moment and then meekly asked his grandfather, 'Which wolf wins?'

The old Cherokee replied, 'The one you feed.'"

Worry can arise in unexpected places. For me, it manifests itself through a busy schedule. I'm always striving to do more and be more. It is difficult to step back and look at the big picture. Yet, I know I am opposing faith when succumbing to worry. Below are four coping mechanisms I've found helpful to combat fear. Consider using one when worry takes center stage in your life.

1. Focus on the here and now:

It is so easy to get distracted with all the noise filling our lives. Americans collectively—across all age groups—check their phones eight billion times daily[4]. It's rare to walk into a restaurant and see two or more people at a table exclusively focused on each other. How did we get to this place as a society? We say we love our family and want to spend more time together, yet our actions prove otherwise.

The solution? Create and seize opportunities to be more present. Take your kids out to the park or grab a treat and just focus on them. Pick a time when you do not feel pressured to rush back home.

2. Confide in someone:
Letting internal worry fill our minds is a vicious cycle. When you worry about one thing, it's natural to think about something else. For example, I was worried about my son's speech delay and was concerned he may have autism. Next, I worried he wouldn't be comfortable in a traditional preschool. The list goes on.

Luckily, my husband, Bryan, easily lives in the present and accepts the things he cannot change. I turn to him when another vicious cycle of worry surfaces. Confiding in Bryan is healing.

We are meant for partnership. Whether it is your spouse or best friend, you need to express your concerns to someone who will help you see things from another vantage point—without judgment. He or she can reframe your perspective.

3. Pray about it:
God is the source of life and all that is good. Offering concerns to Jesus through prayer instills an inner sense of peace. And you do not have to be in a church to pray. Instead, find a quiet place free from distraction. This could be your bedroom or backyard. Quiet produces calm and calm leads to peace. Peace brings us into the present moment and helps us tune out past failures or future worries.

4. Become a problem-solver:
Because we cannot control external events, we need to become excellent problem-solvers. Using my earlier example,

I cannot control whether my son has autism. But I can take him to a specialist for evaluation. If the diagnosis is made, I can see to it that he gets the best possible therapy services and plan financially for them. Those things *are* within my reach.

Moving past fear requires strength, and Alli Worthington's book, *Fierce Faith*[5], is a great resource specifically for women who struggle with fear. She discusses the five unhealthy ways we respond to fear, common types of fear (i.e. rejection, failure, betrayal), and battle plans to fight fear.

Of the ways we typically respond to fear, the one that most resonated with me is busyness. I am a mother of three boys, small business owner, wife, daughter, sister, friend, and volunteer. One of the mothers from my son's baseball team often says she just doesn't know how I do it, how I seemingly have it all together.

Truthfully, I don't have it all together. Faith allows me to put trust in the Lord, that He will open doors of opportunity that need to be opened and shut those that are not a valuable use of time. Faith also beckons me to rely on Bryan. He cleans the dishes, coaches our sons' sports teams, and listens empathetically. When the busy pace of life seems out of control, lean into faith.

The concepts of faith and fear are closely tied to mindset. In a scarcity mindset, you are operating from a needy place where you are constantly concerned there will never be "enough." With the abundance mindset, you see the potential to move beyond present circumstances and place hope in a brighter future.

If you have been stuck with a scarcity mindset in the past, I challenge you to start fresh with this book and instead operate from a place of abundance. There is plenty of wealth to go around.

You Were Made for More

Let's do an exercise. Put this book down, close your eyes, and take two deep breaths. Then open your eyes.

Feel better?

There are great plans for your life. You are blessed.

Read that again.

There are great plans for your life. You are blessed.

As Carrie Gress says in *Nudging Conversations*, "Talents are gifts that God gives us to enjoy, but we enjoy them even more once they're shared. Every gift we have been given is meant not just for ourselves, but to be passed along to others."

Use your gifts to help friends, family, and others in your community. The first half of this book focuses on habits and behaviors that directly impact you, while the second half of the book discusses the impact you have on others—family, friends, your community, and even the world.

Money is only one piece of the equation. Think about the other forms of capital, or wealth, you have and how to use them to help people around you. If you see an injustice, take a stand. Buy a meal for a homeless person. Invest in a company that provides clean water globally. Spread joy!

Chapter Two

Your Past Isn't a Script for Your Future

I'm an accidental entrepreneur. You know how some people grow up in an environment surrounded by a parent or other family member who runs their own business? I didn't have that. As a young girl, I aspired to be a ballerina and music teacher. In my wildest dreams, I never could have imagined that I would be here—an entrepreneur and author.

My last day at the wealth management firm in 2013 was excruciatingly hard. I spent seven years of my life working in a traditional office environment with a clearly defined promotion plan. A strong desire to spend more time with my family didn't alleviate my nervousness about giving up a career that made me feel valued and appreciated.

It was really difficult to move forward into unchartered territory. There were too many unknowns. I had to name the emotion before I could process it: fear.

Whether it is fear of the unknown or a crisis of confidence, change requires a positive viewpoint. The way you think about yourself and your surroundings impacts your methods of learning, reactions to stress, levels of resiliency, and health.

Moving past fear into a bold beginning involves a shift of perspective.

Abundance Mindset

Steven Covey's 1989 bestseller The Seven Habits of Highly Effective People[1] coined the term "abundance mentality." An abundance mindset helps you:

- Create meaningful life experiences.
- Pursue new, interesting opportunities.
- Live a full and satisfying life.
- Find happiness even amid struggle.
- Feel inspired and creative.

True transformation requires an abundance mindset. If you foster an abundance mentality, you see the potential to move beyond present circumstances and have hope in a brighter future. By contrast, a person operating under the scarcity mindset is consistently concerned that there will never be enough and typically feels like a victim. Emotionally, an abundance mindset makes you feel empowered and engaged while a scarcity mindset causes frustration and a sense of being overwhelmed.

The Chopra Center[2] offers several suggestions to move into an abundance mentality, including:

1. Become aware of your thoughts through mindfulness:
Notice the types of thoughts circulating your head and make a conscious effort to shift towards abundance.

2. **Practice gratitude:**
Keep a gratitude journal, recording at least 10 items daily.

3. **Recognize the unlimited possibilities:**
Focus can be incredibly powerful but also unhelpful if your focus is too narrow and you fail to notice other possibilities.

4. **Cultivate and share your passions and purpose:**
Serve others by sharing your unique gifts and providing value.

5. **Think about what is going right:**
Human brains are wired to notice the bad more easily than the good. Take a holistic approach and play to your strengths.

We have the highest living standards of any generation in history. Our World in Data shows how global living conditions are changing. Poverty, illiteracy, and childhood mortality rates have dropped significantly since 1950. Political freedoms stemming from democracy and postsecondary education rates have soared.

Yet 90 percent of people think the world isn't getting better.[3] The media focuses on bad events such as terrorist attacks, natural disasters, and mass shootings. It's quite rare to see any news channel spend more than five minutes of a 30-minute show on "feel good" segments. We don't get to see our everyday heroes on TV or in the newspapers; police officers, firefighters, teachers, and missionaries make the headlines for conflict and controversy, not when things are business as usual.

Despite the good work happening in our neighborhoods and communities worldwide, 1 in 10 people today still live in extreme poverty[3]. To solve big problems like poverty, we need to stop living in isolation and collaborate. Get behind a cause and garner support from others who are interested in advancing the same cause.

When you operate from a place of abundance, it means you are open to change. Any prior mistakes can be acknowledged and treated as a learning experience. They shouldn't prevent you from reaching goals in the future.

My client, Sara, had over $120,000 in student loan debt when we first started working together. She was paying high interest rates, and her monthly student loan payments totaled nearly $2,000. Her goal was to pay off all student loan debt within five years. Although she and her husband, Jim, earned good salaries, they felt burdened by her student loan debt. Both of them were committed to change and operated from an abundance mindset.

Together, we formulated a plan to aggressively pay down the remaining student loans. Originally, Jim and Sara's home mortgage balance totaled $180,000 at a 4.125 percent fixed rate. We refinanced the mortgage—increasing the principal balance but reducing the fixed rate. This allowed the couple to pay down approximately $52,000 of student loan balances, which in turn lowered Sara's student loan debt payments to about $1,000 monthly. Any extra cash was applied to student loan principal, and she had NO student loan debt two years ahead of schedule! Sara and Jim were also able to put money into their savings account while they worked to reduce the student loan balances.

Clearly, this couple started with ambitious goals and quickly surpassed them. In fact, they added over $100,000 of financial net worth to their joint balance sheet in a single year. Jim and Sara's abundance mindset, laser-like focus, and prudent financial decisions worked to their advantage.

The Power of Goal Setting

Mindset and goal setting are intertwined. A crucial piece of the goal setting process is reflection.

Jenni Catron, author of *The 4 Dimensions of Extraordinary Leadership,* shared some of her year-end reflection questions with me. She suggests that you think about your life in the context of four main areas: Spiritual, relational, personal, and vocational. As you consider the last quarter or year, what are your favorite memories in each category? Where did you grow as a person? What changes can you make in the future?

During the reflection process, it may be better for you to focus on the pain first and then the strength you used to overcome that pain. Reflecting on the positive or negative works. It's simply a matter of preference. The key is to use the past as a learning tool. When you are done with the reflection stage and ready to define future goals, consider the SMART framework. Make your goals:

- Specific
- Measurable
- Achievable
- Relevant
- Time-Bound

Suppose you want to increase your family's financial net worth by $20,000 in 2020. Consider incorporating the following principles:

1. **Believe the Possibility.** Start with an abundance mindset and identify self-limiting beliefs that may

have held you back in the past. Develop a simple mantra that you repeat verbally every day, such as "I am worthy of a bright financial future." Even if you've struggled with debt in the past, don't let that hold you back.

2. **Determine Your Why.** Figure out why this goal is truly meaningful to you. Will it help you to retire one year early? Are you saving for a big trip the following year? When the goal seems out of reach, reconnect with your why.

3. **Design Your Future.** Work through the SMART framework, establishing both achievement and habit goals. Achievement goals are focused on the outcome, and habit goals are mini versions that support the broader goal. Your achievement goal is to increase your family's financial net worth by $20,000 by December 31, 2020. Perhaps one habit goal is to contribute $1,000 monthly to your 401(k) plan and $600 monthly to your emergency or opportunity fund, which will be outlined in Chapter 5. Saving $1,600 per month for a year means you're at $19,200. The additional $800 of your big $20,000 goal could be investment appreciation within the 401(k) plan.

4. **Cut the Goal in Half.** Maybe $20,000 truly is out of reach. Would cutting the goal in half to $10,000 make the difference between achieving your goal and letting it disintegrate? Your original goal was $20K by December 31. Perhaps a compromise is $10K by September 30. The beauty of goals is that they can be revised. Ninety-two percent of New Year's

resolutions fail within a matter of weeks, according to Jon Acuff's book, *Finish*[4]. Do you want to be in that 92 percent? Rightsizing the goal may keep you in the elite 8 percent.

5. **Use Data to Celebrate Progress.** Know ahead of time what rewards you will use to celebrate small wins. Make your incentives meaningful and find a tracking tool to monitor progress. Manually updating an Excel file on a regular basis allows you to see how far you've come. If you work with a financial advisor, ask to see quarterly updates.

SMART goal setting is helpful but not the only ingredient for success.

"In their hearts humans plan their course, but the LORD establishes their steps."

– Proverbs 16: 9

We can have the best laid plans. But if we aren't open to following God's will, we aren't really fulfilling our purpose in life as Christians. Goals are great, but we should not follow them if they entail walking down a path that contradicts our higher purpose.

Wealth Building Behaviors

Beyond mindset and clearly established goals, what does it take to build long-term financial wealth? Dr. Thomas J. Stanley spent years researching this question and reported his findings in *The Millionaire Next Door*[5] in 1996. In his survey of more than 14,000 affluent American households, Stanley concluded that households can become wealthy without six- or seven-figure salaries.

Dr. Stanley unexpectedly passed away in 2015, and his daughter Dr. Sarah Fallaw recently published *The Next Millionaire Next Door*[6]. Dr. Fallaw confirms that many of the behaviors identified in Stanley's research continue to play a significant role in wealth accumulation, and she offers assurance that it is possible to change behaviors.

Hard work, diligence, frugality, and time management are more important than salary alone. Choice of spouse, career, and location also play special roles. Wealth and hyper-consumption do not go hand in hand. Frugality, or consistently living below your means, is the better choice.

Frugality

I encourage you to read Chapter 4, Budget Isn't a Dirty Word, if frugality is a real struggle for your household. Remember, you are not the only one who is challenged by this! If impatience gets the best of you, here are some general guidelines to follow:

1. **Start a budget now.**
   Whether it's an Excel file or online app like *You Need a Budget*, everyone can benefit from a budget. It helps you track income (money coming in) and expenses (cash going out). You may need a few

months of data before you get a feel for actual spending activity and that's OK. A budget is your baseline.

2. **Monitor your budget.**
   Resolutions often fail because we do not revisit them. The same holds true for budgets. You cannot have a "set it and forget it" mentality if you want to make any progress towards goals. Rather, set a recurring appointment to revisit your situation and make required adjustments.

3. **Focus on what really matters.**
   Does a specific expense improve your physical, mental, or emotional health? One of my clients was scared to tell me that she has a personal trainer. Regular meetings with her trainer enhance her overall well-being. Personal training is an investment in her physical and emotional health that results in fewer medical emergencies and doctor visits. When she was looking to make budget cuts, I suggested she continue with the personal trainer but perhaps meet him less frequently and focus on other areas to cut. Home-cooked meals are generally healthier and less expensive than eating out, so I also encouraged her to revisit the cost of dining out.

4. **Consider a mindset shift.**
   Rather than viewing frugal decisions as constraints, reflect on the long-term progress you're making in pursuit of financial freedom. Positive thoughts beget remarkable results. Remember the abundance mindset we discussed at the beginning of this

chapter? Use it to reframe any negative connotation you have around budgeting.

Discipline & Monitoring

Psychologist and author, Carol Dweck[7], popularized the term "growth mindset" in her book, *Mindset: The New Psychology of Success*.

> "In a growth mindset, people believe that their most basic abilities can be developed through dedication and hard work—brains and talent are just the starting point," Dweck writes. "This view creates a love of learning and a resilience that is essential for great accomplishment."

The correlation between growth mindset and findings in *The Next Millionaire Next Door* are astonishing. Clearly, diligence is one characteristic that will help you achieve goals. It is no wonder that several of the millionaires featured in Stanley's book are entrepreneurs. They are willing to fail fast, brush themselves off, and try again.

Another component to building wealth is effective allocation of time, energy, and money. You should have a good grasp of where your money is going and how it is either enhancing or detracting from your lifestyle. Establishing a budget is one thing but monitoring that budget is an entirely different exercise. If you are supporting charitable causes, ensure the charitable organizations wisely use that money.

Although you should not check your investment portfolio on a daily basis, it is beneficial to have a general idea of its direction. Setting a financial independence goal is great but ignoring a 20 percent market decline will defer that goal significantly. Instead, set a monthly or quarterly reminder to review your budget, financial statement of net worth, and upcoming goals.

Wealth builders often conduct deeper searches for quality advisors—accountants, attorneys, and investment consultants—and meet with those advisors more frequently. They take a long-term approach to investing and are not looking for the next hot stock tip. Rather, wealth accumulators acknowledge their areas of weakness and hire other experienced professionals to assist with detailed tax or investment questions.

If you are married, one of you may be more naturally inclined to monitor your financial status. That's perfectly fine! Just try to include your spouse in the discussions. One of my clients pays meticulous attention to his family's budget and investment mix, while his wife is nauseated at the sight of spreadsheets. Although her interests clearly lie in other areas, she is committed to attending our meetings so long as we discuss high-level aspirations instead of nitty-gritty details.

Independence

Research from *The Next Millionaire Next Door* also indicates that financial independence is critical to accumulating wealth. Prodigious builders of wealth are not as concerned with social status. They are willing to drive used cars and live in older homes. In fact, many of them shy away from luxury purchases. I once worked with a client who had more than five million dollars of investable assets. She lived in a modest $300,000 home in a small farm town and never spent more than $150,000 annually, which represented the income generated from her investment portfolio.

Another client couple, Bob and Sue, live on approximately one-third of Bob's physician salary. The other two-thirds goes toward savings, charitable giving, and tax obligations. They foster financial independence in their 17-year-old daughter by having her pay for half of all college costs (tuition, housing, books, and other fees).

Related to independence is the concept of economic outpatient care. According to Dr. Stanley in *The Millionaire Next Door,* "In general, the more dollars adult children receive, the fewer they accumulate, while those who are given fewer dollars accumulate more." Economic outpatient care is a slippery slope, and here's an example to illustrate it:

> Mom and dad have a lot of money, so they start giving Suzy money to fund her lifestyle as a young adult. Before you know it, Suzy is accustomed to getting $1,000 a month from her parents. She marries Steve and continues to receive this generous stipend. Suzy and her husband Steve have kids, and they must have the perfect house in the best school district for their children. Her parents assist with the house down payment. Two years later, Steve loses his job and Suzy is a stay-at-home mom. Suzy's parents cannot stomach the idea of getting rid of the house, so they make the mortgage payments until Steve finds employment. And so, the vicious cycle continues.

Hopefully, you haven't witnessed economic outpatient care to the same extent as my example. But it was exaggerated for a reason. Economic outpatient care is the opposite of financial independence. If you are receiving handouts from a parent or relative, figure out a plan to end the cycle. Preferably, use the cold turkey method. Let the person know that you are gracious for their past support but that you want to forge a new future. Or, if that conversation is too uncomfortable, ensure you are wisely investing the gift. Consider it a "bonus" rather than income to allocate to living expenses.

Cardinal Virtues

If you agree that wealth isn't just about the money, how do we take these concepts from Dr. Fallaw's book, *The Next Millionaire Next Door*[6], and parlay them into other facets of wealth? Let's investigate human and social capital in the context of virtues.

St. Thomas Aquinas refers to the four cardinal virtues as prudence, temperance, courage, and justice.

> **Prudence** is an intellectual aptitude that allows us to act in accordance with our moral standards.
> **Temperance** is synonymous with moderation.
> **Courage** restrains and even combats our fears.
> **Justice** is focused on the welfare of the entire community and governs our actions according to the common good.

Prudence, temperance, and courage govern our individual behaviors, while justice pertains to our relationships with others.

The financial discipline exhibited by wealth builders in Dr. Fallaw's research mimics Aquinas' virtue of prudence. You may not want to spend an hour monthly monitoring the family budget or investment strategies, but you do it anyway because you know it will lead to a better outcome. One of my former clients acknowledged a spending issue but didn't make progress because she was unwilling to dedicate the time and energy into monitoring it. Her lack of prudence in this regard spilled into other areas of life. She worked hard in a position for little pay and sacrificed time with her family. It was a dangerous spiral. Prudence and discipline would have helped her tremendously. Yet, she was unwilling to change.

Temperance and frugality are closely intertwined. People who live frugally still own material possessions. But they accumulate those possessions in moderation and know when to give them away. One of the greatest lessons my parents taught me as a young girl is needs versus wants. The next time you are contemplating a major purchase, pose this question to yourself, "Is this a need or a want?"

If your microwave is broken and you're standing in front of a new microwave, it's a need. When you buy that new microwave, get rid of the old one. If, on the other hand, the object is a want, walk away (or leave it in your online shopping cart) and return after a few minutes. If upon seeing the item a second time you still think it is a good idea—maybe because it's a reward for reaching a goal—then consider buying it.

Instant gratification deters us from reaching goals. Psychologist and Stanford professor, Walter Mischel, conducted an experiment on delayed gratification in the late 1960s and early 1970s that was later dubbed the "marshmallow" experiment. A child was given the option between one small reward immediately or two small rewards after a short wait. Children who exhibited self-control and waited for two rewards had better life outcomes in school, health, and other areas.

Nonetheless, there is modern-day controversy over this earlier marshmallow study. Behavioral Scientist's 2018 article[8] points to the importance of affluence in follow-up studies. People living in poverty focus on short-term needs due to scarce resources and uncertainty of the future. Therefore, impoverished children are more likely to take the marshmallow right away.

Most adults are able to delay gratification. We wait to eat dessert until after finishing dinner. The kids are safely tucked in bed before we relax from a hard day's work. But it doesn't mean we are perfect.

If moderation represents the middle and overindulgence is one extreme, the polar opposite extreme is excessive thrift. Wearing shoes until the soles are falling off or keeping clothing with multiple holes isn't wise. Get rid of the item if it becomes a safety issue or no longer works.

Moderation is "middle of the road" behavior. As a parent, you likely are not taking weekly skydiving expeditions. Similarly, drinking in excess at a child's birthday party is not only embarrassing to you but also to your entire family. Temperance benefits you in many ways.

Courage is especially important if you are moving from a scarcity mindset towards an abundance mentality. It provides a battle plan against fear. This virtue is critical for behavior change.

You make a million decisions a day. How many of those decisions do you consider courageous? I'm not proposing you make unwise decisions strictly based on excitement or adventure. Rather, focus on the big decisions that will truly move the needle. Your past isn't a script for your future. You can always forge a new path.

Justice and independence are connected as well. If you rely on someone else, stewardship is probably hard for you. God freely gives us gifts. Relying on others' handouts means you cannot share those gifts with others. For instance, if someone breaks the law and serves time in jail, he cannot share his unique gifts with people outside of prison.

Independence may appear selfish on the surface. But it actually enables you to give and share on a whole new level. As you'll see later in the book, financial independence is a goal for many people and it represents a time when you no longer *have* to work for pay. Sharing your gifts without any hidden agenda benefits your entire community. And you don't need to be financially independent. You can begin sharing wealth now!

Chapter Three

Lead with Values

Have you ever had one of those God moments? A time when you vividly felt His presence? You don't have to see Him to know He's right there, orchestrating it all.

I've had quite a few over the last couple of years. I think the more we open our hearts to a relationship with Jesus, the more opportunities he has to speak into our souls.

My most recent "God moment" happened in July 2018. My family and I had returned from a three-month hiatus in Spain a few months earlier, and my husband, Bryan, was knee-deep in his job search.

Part of the Spain adventure was to give Bryan time and space to think about a new career, but he also sought comfort. Bryan had gone through lengthy interview processes with several prospective employers and we were willing to relocate our family if it meant he had a steady job. By God's design, Bryan didn't receive a single job offer.

We spent a hot July weekend at the Lake of the Ozarks. It should have been fun but there was a dark cloud hanging over us. Our cash cushion was quickly dwindling. I usually had a steady stream of new prospective WorthyNest® clients but summer was slow.

One day, my sons woke up early and wanted to get into the lake. Bryan slept as I watched the boys splash in murky water. After they tired themselves out, my oldest and youngest sons went inside to change while my middle son let me wrap him tightly in a towel. It was just the two of us and that rarely happens.

As my son and I sat quietly on the lawn chair dockside, I looked out into the water. I suddenly had a song to sing, a song I hadn't sung in years—"Open the Eyes of My Heart." I very gently started:

> "Open the eyes of my heart Lord,
> Open the eyes of my heart,
> I want to see you…,
> I want to see you…."

I must have repeated the refrain at least 50 times. The sunlight hit the water perfectly, and it looked as if the water was dancing. A warm breeze enveloped my body, and I knew God was there with us. I thought this must be a slice of what heaven is like.

I've held onto that moment. God assured me our family would be OK, regardless of Bryan's job situation.

The car ride home that day also was meaningful. Bryan and I revisited a conversation we'd had more than a year earlier. We discussed whether he should pursue a position in corporate recruiting.

Bryan and I both grew up with loving parents who like to play things "safe." They believe you should work hard, get a college degree in something that pays well, and do that for the rest of your life. Plenty of people follow that path.

Bryan's prior career was "safe." It was a steady paycheck. Transitioning into corporate recruiting was an unsteady path. The initial 40 percent pay cut and commission-based compensation structure meant a big leap of faith. Yet, Bryan's personality tests revealed he would be better suited for such a role. After five months of grueling interviews at other companies, Bryan finally stepped into a corporate recruiting position.

Values Are Everything

This story highlights one of our family's core values: Adaptability. Just because you've been doing something for a long time doesn't mean you must continue doing it. Rather, ponder these questions:

1. Is the activity or job bringing joy to me and my family?
2. What would I do instead if I gave this up?
3. Would discontinuing it bring lasting happiness?

Often, the riskier option is inaction. And if you're worried that happiness isn't biblical, you're mistaken. Just read Jennifer Dukes Lee's book, *The Happiness Dare*.

Dukes Lee hits the nail on the head:

> "I flipped back to a familiar verse in Zephaniah: 'The Lord your God is with you, the Mighty Warrior who saves. He will take great delight in you; in his love he will no longer rebuke you but will rejoice over you with singing.' What kind of

God delights over his people with singing? Our happy God. That's who."

Happiness and holiness needn't be on opposite ends of the spectrum.

Earlier, I asked you to reflect on your purpose and acknowledge that the past isn't a script for your future. If you went through those exercises, you may have a clear idea of core values—principles that align with your moral ethos. Now it is time to revisit those values (or start from scratch if you need more time now to give it serious thought).

Some of the core Christian values include:
- Humility
- Gratitude
- Wisdom
- Grace
- Hope
- Faith
- Love
- Service
- Trust
- Compassion

Which words resonate most deeply with you? Are there other core values not included in the list above?

Beyond adaptability, I've thought a lot about our family's values. To live an abundant, prosperous life, I think many of our values contradict ones traditionally espoused by society.

For instance, we live in a materialistic world. People wait in long lines to buy the latest iPhone, even when their current one is only a year old. Or they sacrifice time with family after Thanksgiving to be the first in the store for Black Friday deals.

Living a simple, uncluttered life is the opposite of hyper-consumerism. The minimalist movement is especially appealing for this reason. But believe me, I'm a work-in-progress. With three young kids, it's quite challenging to model simplicity when friends' parents provide multiple toys each Christmas while we insist on gift cards to family-friendly places. Joshua Becker[1] says it well:

> "Every increased possession adds increased anxiety into our lives. Everything we own takes up physical space in our home and mental space in our mind. Our possessions require maintenance and cleaning, creating a cause-and-effect relationship between our excess possessions and our overall lack of time, energy, and focus."

Responsibility is another value in our household. We take responsibility for our actions and have consequences if rules aren't followed. How often do you see someone blaming another person for his or her actions? Maybe it's the recovering perfectionist in me, but I'm quick to acknowledge when I've made a mistake and ask for forgiveness.

On a similar note, we teach our sons that cheating and stealing are wrong because honesty is the best policy. Many people think of shoplifting as inconsequential, but it could set the stage for further criminal actions. If a first-time offender is caught, it's a misdemeanor that may be dismissed after going through a court-supervised community service program.[2] Harsher punishments to "petty" crimes such as shoplifting may curb the behavior once and for all.

Another family value is tolerance. We accept others for who they are and don't resort to violence when there is a disagreement, especially a political one.

Moving beyond tolerance to acceptance and (eventually) appreciation is even more admirable. Anyone who espouses diversity and inclusion will tell you to not only accept people's differences but to actually celebrate them, too! Generosity, then, becomes the ideal. We should be generous with our time, talent, and treasure to help those who may not be as advantaged as us.

"The King will reply, 'Truly I tell you, whatever you did for one of the least of these brothers and sisters of mine, you did for me.'"

– Matthew 25:40

Patience is another common value. With technological advances, everything is on-demand. Want to skip commercials on TV? You can pay for a premium service that lets you record and fast forward through shows. No wonder Netflix is such a success for movie buffs and TV fanatics.

And finally, courage. It is very similar to adaptability. When you make a significant change, you must move past the fear of failure. That certainly isn't easy. It involves surrender and putting your trust in Jesus, knowing he will carry you.

This can be hard if you're a planner or perfectionist like me. You want to look into the future, envision a scenario, and research it extensively. You explore the possibilities. When you get stuck on the hamster wheel of continuous planning, it may remove joy from your life.

Here is a recap of other core values you may want to consider adding to your list:
- Simplicity
- Responsibility
- Honesty
- Tolerance
- Appreciation
- Generosity
- Patience
- Courage

Instilling Great Financial Values

Early experiences shape our perspectives. If money was scarce during your childhood, you may have one of two reactions as an adult: 1) hold on tight to every penny, or 2) spend freely so your kids can have a "better" future.

Unfortunately, both approaches represent extremes. Ideally, you'll find a compromise where you can save, share, and spend in accordance with your overarching values.

If you grew up in a household where money was never a concern, you may feel your parents robbed you of financial independence. Financial handouts at an early age foster a reliance on parental support for years to come, and it's hard to break that habit as an adult. Even if you can afford to pay for your child's material desires, it's prudent to have your child earn income and make their own budgeting decisions.

One of my college friends, Sam, never worked for pay until his first job after college. He had a hard time securing a position because employers often emphasize prior work experience. He had none, not even an unpaid internship or part-time summer job. Relying entirely on parental handouts makes financial independence more difficult for children later in life.

What Kind of Children Do You Want to Raise?

Beyond passing down values to your kids, remember that you are your child's best teacher. Here are five financial techniques I'm using with my sons in an effort to raise them to be great adults:

1. Don't spoil.

I can't tell you the number of times my nine-year-old has asked for things. For instance, I'm making a Target run, and he gladly offers to come with me. Minutes into our visit, I remember his real intention for joining me: Legos or Pokémon cards.

If you are faced with a similar situation, resist the urge to say "yes" to every request. You can spoil your child with hugs and kisses, but don't buy everything they want (even if you have the financial resources to do it). Instead, have a genuine conversation with your child. Help him understand the difference between wants and needs. Also see if he is willing to pay for a portion or all of the item's cost. Ron

Lieber's *NYT* bestseller, *The Opposite of Spoiled*[3], offers other suggestions, too.

At Target, I tell my son that he must use his money or gift cards if he wants to buy any toys. Likewise, in advance of his sibling's athletic event, I make it clear that my son can pick a granola bar or other snack from home and a water bottle. Otherwise, he is solely responsible for paying for the food or drink he buys at the game. This keeps both of us happy. He often gets what he wants but learns basic budgeting concepts simultaneously.

Give your child a chance to earn money. Older children may be able to earn money by raking leaves, mowing lawns, pet sitting, babysitting, cleaning the house, or finding other part-time employment.

2. Instill great habits early.

Want to teach young kids how to allocate money they receive as gifts or by operating a lemonade stand? Consider three clear jars or plastic containers labeled "Share," "Save," and "Spend."

I first heard of this concept several years ago through Nathan Dungan, founder of Share Save Spend[4]. He suggested having your kids divide any new money they get equally among the three jars. For example, $15 would be divided into three jars of five dollars each. The share jar is used for charitable giving, while the save jar eventually gets deposited in a bank account. Spend is self-explanatory.

Since money temperaments vary, recognize that your child may want to put all of the money into a single jar. Come to an agreement where your child can direct more money to a single jar and make smaller contributions to the other two jars. My nine-year-old wants to spend, so we agreed to put half of his money into the spend jar and then the other half into save and share jars.

Once your child masters the three-jar concept, consider adding a fourth jar to subdivide savings into medium and long-term goals. Medium savings goals may be an expensive outing or toy, while long-term savings relate to college and beyond.

3. Give them a leg up.

Get a piggy bank! I don't know how it happens, but my kids seem to find coins all over the place. We may use the share, save, and spend jars for larger denominations but any coins they collect go straight into the piggy bank.

I love seeing my oldest son deposit his piggy bank full of coins at the brick-and-mortar bank. We discuss how the deposit is going to earn interest (a.k.a. "free money") just for sitting there. My middle son and I sort the coins before the bank trip. These two small actions—sorting and depositing—work wonders in giving my kids a leg up in life, financially speaking.

If you want to take budgeting concepts digitally, consider FamZoo[5]. They offer prepaid cards and a family finance app for kids, teens, and parents. ProActive[6] is ideal if you struggle with cash flow management personally, want a digital "envelope" budget system, and need to monitor your child's money on the same app.

4. Save for future opportunities.

Saving for college is an important long-term goal but not the only objective. If you want your child to invest early, companies like Stockpile[7] are making it easy to buy fractional shares of recognizable brands such as Disney and Amazon. Be cognizant of transaction fees, though; they currently charge $0.99 per trade, and this may represent a large chunk of the purchase price if you're buying a small number of shares.

Worthy[8] connects qualified borrowers (i.e. small business owners) to individual investors. As an investor, you earn 5 percent interest on $10 bonds. I'm personally not planning on buying a bunch of $10 bonds but think this might be a good tactic to try with my oldest son if he becomes frustrated by the traditional bank's paltry interest rate.

5. Prioritize service.

Do you volunteer for a particular organization or is there an opportunity through church to lend a helping hand? Consider bringing your child along (if permitted). Tithing is great, but it strictly pertains to finances. We are also called to graciously give our time and talents.

It may be difficult to find volunteer slots for young children but a plethora of opportunities usually open in middle school and beyond. Consider your child's passions and abilities. If he has a heart for pets, he may want to volunteer at the animal shelter. She may opt to organize nonperishable food items for a pantry. Adopting a family in need during the holidays could allow children of all ages to be involved.

Zach Tucker of Good Meets World, a social impact organization based in St. Louis, shares a few other ways to do good with your children:

a. **Dine together at a restaurant that publicly gives back.** Restaurants will often post the charitable cause on the menu or a table flyer.
b. **Tour a nonprofit facility together.** Wings of Hope and Operation Food Search are two organizations in greater St. Louis that offer family tours. Wings of Hope makes life-saving medical flights possible for children in need worldwide, while Operation Food Search provides healthy meals to families who would otherwise go hungry.
c. **Birthday parties.** In lieu of gifts, ask family members and friends to bring nonperishable food items or donate money to your child's charity of choice. An added bonus: you can immediately clear the clutter and won't have to find a place for new toys.

All of these suggestions instill positive values in your children that may help them their entire lives. Volunteering shows your children that they can make a meaningful impact regardless of how much money they have.

When my two older sons and I volunteered for Kids in Hunger to benefit children in Haiti, we discussed how a single small bag of food would feed a family of six for one day. I further explained that this may be the only meal a family has that day. Our table of eight volunteers managed to make and package 180 meals in less than two hours. Want to know something else enlightening? My oldest and middle sons had the best behavior I've seen in a long time. They focused on a task greater than themselves, and it made all the difference.

What are you called to teach your kids today? This week? This month?

Which values will you (and your spouse, if married) prioritize in the year ahead? Which ones will you share with your children? If you like to plan things, maybe you can have a month-by-month value theme. The theme might be compassion this month and honesty the following month.

Multiple shared values are wonderful, but having too many values could confuse your children or make it harder to master one. Select five or six core values instead. Think about the ones that guide your relationships and daily interactions. Clearly defining your values is critical to the goal-setting process.

We've already established that you were made for more and that your past isn't a script for your future. At this point, you should also have a concise list of family values that guide your behaviors and goals. Next, let's explore financial concepts, including budgets, savings, debt, and investing.

Chapter Four

Budget Isn't a Dirty Word

I ran into a friend while grocery shopping with my sons one day. She immediately asked what happened to my forehead.

I'll admit it...I'm very uncoordinated. So clumsy, in fact, that I was bending down underneath a table at a surprise party and stood up, hitting my forehead on the top of the table. It hurt badly! But I shrugged it off and continued on with the party, forgetting it was even there. Six days later at the grocery store, the bump and bruise looked worse than ever, but I was fine.

The point of this story? Looks can be deceiving.

Someone may be driving a BMW, Mercedes, or other luxury car but also have loads of debt. On the opposite extreme, you may find a multimillionaire in her seventies who lives in a very modest home and only wears clothes she purchased 20 years ago. We each have choices when it comes to money. How we display those choices has no correlation to what is actually happening.

Resist the temptation to keep up with your neighbors or other parents. Focus less on what other people think or how you've spent money in the past. Recognize that your worth isn't defined by the car you drive or home in which you live. **Prioritize the items that matter to you now.** Do you want to send your children to private school? Is charitable giving a high priority? Include these important items in your budget.

Downsizing Is Difficult

Think back to the last time you made a big purchase. Was it a home? A car? Furniture? Try to recreate what you felt at that moment. Emotionally and financially, it's a big decision. You don't want to make a wrong choice.

Not too long ago, my husband Bryan and I were researching cars. He bought a Kia Optima that had the "cutting-edge" feature of remote keyless entry. Thinking it was unnecessary at the time but nice nonetheless, he bought the car and didn't give it another thought. When it came time to for me to get a new vehicle, though, Bryan urged me to get one equipped with the same feature. Why? Because he upsized, and his expectations followed suit.

His love for remote keyless entry convinced me to seek this feature in my new vehicle. With three young kids to cart around in an SUV, I also really enjoy the automatic trunk door lift—it allows us to store groceries, strollers, and sports equipment without a lot of physical effort.

We've created a monster. Even though we both plan to keep our vehicles for a long time, it will be excruciatingly hard to ever return to an old-fashioned key or manual trunk release. Experiencing the benefits of the remote keyless entry and automatic trunk release makes it difficult to downsize in the future.

Although the above example was minor, the point is still the same. *It is always easier to "upsize" than to "downsize."* It's no wonder that cashiers at McDonald's always ask if you want to supersize your fries and drink. If you say yes to the offer now, you'll need more self-restraint when ordering a Value Meal in the future. Living below your means creates better possibilities down the road.

Let's suppose you have one child, both you and your spouse work outside the home, and you plan to have more kids. You want to move and are preapproved for a $250,000 home. Consider the advantages if you purchase a $200,000 home instead. Saving $40,000 for a 20 percent down payment is easier than $50,000. Your monthly mortgage payment and annual property tax bills will be lower. Those savings could go directly into home renovations or business start-up capital. **Think of the opportunities, not the sacrifices, you create with a frugal decision.**

Budget Isn't a Bad Word

OK, I need you to be honest for a moment. When you hear the word budget, what comes to mind?

It's no surprise that the term budget often has many negative connotations. It implies you know how much you spend each month, and you then feel guilty if you don't find a way to control your spending. One of my previous employers spent a great deal of time trying to disguise the word "budget" by using terms like "cash flow management" or "financial independence analysis." Whatever you call it, let's challenge the traditional way of how you view a budget.

A budget is not intrinsically evil. It is a means to formalize your spending patterns and craft financial goals. Since life is not static, those goals will change over time. Your financial goals should be tied to life priorities, too. Below is a mini-chronicle of my budget as an adult and how it has shifted, based on life circumstances.

My budget as a new college graduate was pretty basic and separated into three main categories:

1. **Fixed expenses** (e.g. rent, utilities, and insurance)
2. **Variable expenses** (e.g. food, clothes, and entertainment)
3. **Savings** (e.g. to fund down payment on a home)

Later, living in the Midwest and earning a good salary as a newly minted accountant, there was plenty of wiggle room in my budget for fun expenses like entertainment and recreation.

By the time my husband Bryan and I married, we owned a nice "starter" home and had combined financial resources to create an even bigger cushion. Budget categories remained the same but extra funds went into our savings for a down payment on a larger home in the suburbs.

I continue to use the same budget format from Microsoft Excel that I developed about 15 years ago, yet there are many more line items in each category. With the addition of each child, we had a budget overhaul. When our first son was born in 2009, I knew I would return to work. Saving was relatively easy for us, even with a reduced workload and full-time childcare.

With the arrival of our second son in 2013, I was unsure about returning to paid work since Bryan was working full-time in a professional role and attending a demanding evening MBA program. We must have reviewed our budget at least 100 times to see if we could live solely on my husband's income. **Seriously.** I reluctantly went back to work after our second son's birth but stayed only about eight months.

Leaving my steady position in 2013 was a big shift for our family. We went from financially comfortable to surviving. Spending categories like clothing and entertainment that were selfish indulgences (prior to having kids) were now exclusively focused on our boys. We sought out activities for low or no cost that could be enjoyed as a family. The annual vacation budget amount of $3,000 from 2005 was the same as 2015, but we had to make accommodations for a family of five rather than two. There was little to no wiggle room in this new budget, and that made us very uncomfortable.

To alleviate our financial stress and maintain my professional expertise, I started an accounting firm in 2014. Income from SV CPA Services and WorthyNest® provides the financial breathing room we need maintain a comfortable, but not extravagant, lifestyle. Having a detailed budget has been especially helpful in the last few years as my husband navigated two periods of unemployment.

There is no single budget that

will work for all families.

Depending on your stage of life, level of debt, personal habits, and spouse's habits (if applicable), you may find one budget that will work better than another. Your preferred budget could evolve as you become more financially responsible.

There are two main types of budgets, the envelope budget and the more detailed personal budget.

Envelope Budget

The envelope budget is perfect for those starting on a path to good money management. It is the foundational budget often suggested for new college graduates, but it also can be helpful if you do not have a good idea where your money is going each month. The basic premise of the envelope budget is that you can't spend more than you earn. Under the method, you use only cash or debit cards. No credit cards are allowed. Your *net* paycheck goes into a large master envelope along with three smaller envelopes labeled "Needs," "Savings," and "Fun."

1. NEEDS

In this first envelope, set aside enough money for fixed expenses that must be paid. Examples include rent or mortgage payment, utilities, transportation costs, insurance, groceries, debt service payments, and so on. Aim for no more than 50 percent of your net earnings to go in this envelope.

2. SAVINGS

Next, set a savings goal and put that cash into this other envelope. This is savings outside of any retirement plan. Do NOT use this savings envelope under any circumstance—take this one right to the bank so you can earn interest. It may not be a big dollar amount now, but you'll be amazed at how fast this opportunity fund can grow over time. If 20 percent is too high of a savings goal, start off smaller at 10 percent and work your way up. If you increase the goal by 2 percent each quarter, you'll get to 20 percent in a little over a year.

3. FUN

This final envelope is designed to pay for all those other things you want, such as dining out, memberships, concerts and shows, travel—you get the picture. Once this envelope is empty, that's it. If you have to eat macaroni and cheese each night for a week, so be it. You are NOT allowed to pull from the other envelopes. The savings envelope is for unforeseen events such as a job loss or broken appliances, and needs are true necessities, not wants.

The idea of carrying only cash may not appeal to you since we live in a very tech-savvy age. In theory, you can apply this same concept online but may find it more challenging. Having the physical cash that runs out—if only for a month or two—can be the sobering reality you need to get on track if you are in debt or struggling to make ends meet. Focus on automatic transfers and debit cards if you decide to take the envelope budget online. Do NOT introduce credit cards at this point, as they will only distract you from your goals.

Detailed Personal Budget

For those of you who find the envelope budget too simple, let's discuss the Detailed Personal Budget instead. Below, you'll find a sample budget for a heterosexual married couple where both spouses are employed. Go to redefiningfamilywealth.com/resources to download an electronic copy.

SAMPLE DETAILED BUDGET

	Monthly	Annual
INCOME		
Husband Gross Earnings	_____	_____
Wife Gross Earnings	_____	_____
Other	_____	_____
1. TOTAL GROSS INCOME	_____	_____
EXPENSES		
Rent or Mortgage (P&I)	_____	_____
Utilities (e.g. trash, sewer, A/C, heat)	_____	_____
Cell Phones, TV, Internet	_____	_____
Child Care, if applicable	_____	_____
School, if applicable	_____	_____
Loan Payments	_____	_____
Insurance		
Auto	_____	_____
Life & Supplemental Disability	_____	_____
Other (e.g. homeowners, umbrella)	_____	----------
2. SUBTOTAL: FIXED EXPENSES	_____	_____
Cash (ATM withdrawals)	_____	_____
Charitable Giving	_____	_____
Clothing	_____	_____
Dining Out	_____	_____
Entertainment	_____	_____
Financial Planning	_____	_____
Fitness	_____	_____
Gifts	_____	_____
Groceries	_____	_____

	Monthly	Annual
Home Improvement & Maintenance		
Household/Shopping/Misc.		
Kids Activities (parties, camps, extracurriculars)		
Out-of-Pocket Medical (including copays)		
Pets, if applicable		
Personal Care		
Services (e.g. lawn care, pest control, cleaning)		
Transportation		
Travel & Vacations		

3. SUBTOTAL: DISCRETIONARY EXPENSES

	Monthly	Annual
Income Tax		
Federal		
State & Local		
SS & Medicare		
Other tax		
Real Estate Tax, if applicable		
Personal Property Tax		
Payroll Deductions		
Health Insurance		
Dental and Vision Insurance		
Husband's Retirement Contribution		
Wife's Retirement Contribution		
Other (e.g. additional insurance)		

4. SUBTOTAL: OTHER/ANNUAL

TOTAL EXPENSES

5. SURPLUS/(SHORTFALL)

© 2019 Redefining Family Wealth. All Rights Reserved.

PART 1 – Income

Look at all income sources for you and your spouse (e.g. employment, distributions from investment accounts, outside support, etc.) and list each one separately as a line item. The annual column should be populated first. To be conservative, annual bonuses should be left off the income section. These fluctuating payments will truly represent a bonus because you can pay down debt or add to savings. Just ensure you withhold taxes from this bonus as you do any other wages.

PART 2 – Required Expenses

You may not have a dollar amount for every line item here, but this is intended to be a good starting point. Generally speaking, it is helpful to budget for large annual expenses each month so you do not have to think about a big year-end bill around the holidays. If your mortgage provider offers to escrow real estate tax and home insurance bills, do it. Insurance agencies and private schools typically offer payment plans for a minimal fee to spread out payments over 12 months rather than a single, annual payment. Fixed, required expenses should not exceed 50 percent of gross income.

PART 3 – Discretionary Expenses

Again, you may not have every category filled, but this is meant to give you a point of reference. Feel free to reposition Charitable Giving from Discretionary to Part 2 – Fixed Expenses if you tithe. Discretionary does not mean unnecessary; it simply reflects the variability of the expense.

This third section leaves plenty of wiggle room for your family to prioritize your financial goals.

To determine the monthly amount of discretionary expenses, think about averages. Vacation certainly won't cost $300 every month for 12 months, so consider an annual vacation budget and divide by 12. Medical here represents out-of-pocket expenses. Any employer-sponsored insurance coverage is listed in the following section, Part 4, under Payroll Deductions. Aim to have Discretionary Expenses at or below 30 percent of gross income.

PART 4 – Other/Annual

Refer to paystubs and prior year tax returns to customize this information. Health, dental, and vision insurance coverage should be based on elections you make through your employer. Salary deferral to a company-sponsored plan such as a 401(k) or 403(b) plan is highly recommended. You may even qualify for an employer match. More pre-tax savings leads to a lower tax bill, so high-income taxpayers may benefit from maximizing their retirement contributions. Roth IRA—if you're eligible—or Roth 401(k) contributions are helpful if you are in a lower income tax bracket now than you intend to be in the future.

PART 5 – Surplus, or Net Savings Goal

Your bottom line resides in Section 5. This is the amount you have remaining after all other categories have been filled. If there is a surplus, great! Your next step is to decide together which nonretirement goal(s) to tackle first. Or you could consider increasing your retirement contribution in Part 4, Payroll Deductions section.

If you find yourself with a shortfall, revisit the other sections for errors and see if you are above the suggested percentage guidelines in the Required or Discretionary Expense sections. Do not be discouraged; this is a starting point and can serve as an excellent conversation starter with your spouse as you jointly prioritize goals. You may also want to read Chapter 6 on debt because that is often the culprit for spending more than you earn.

Putting It into Practice

The envelope budget and more detailed budget shown above are not the only types of budgets. Google "sample budget" and you'll find more than enough options. I've always been inclined to save. Even as a young college graduate, I went right into a detailed Excel budget. The envelope budget was unnecessary because I already lived within my means. It is included here because I've seen the envelope budget in action, transforming my clients' lives.

The sample detailed budget closely mimics the budget that my husband and I currently use. You may find something in the "middle" that works well…not quite so many categories but a budget that enables you to use credit cards because you know the bill will be paid in full each month.

If you are frugal and haven't used a formal budget in the past, give it a try. You may find that it sparks conversation with your spouse or challenges you to exceed a monthly savings goal. Perhaps you're financially supporting a young adult. He may not have plans to leave the house or pursue financial independence until you give him a reason. Help him craft a forward-looking budget to understand the types of expenses he'll face when he moves out.

Creating the budget is only the first step of the process. Monitoring the budget is equally, if not more, important. It is hard to know what you are spending on discretionary items such as meals out, household items, and entertainment. You may budget $500 a month for dining out. If your actual cost to dine out is closer to $600 monthly, you need to find another place to trim $100.

If monitoring a budget doesn't come naturally to you, consider an online budgeting tool like Mint or You Need A Budget. Be careful, however, to check the security level of the site before you enter personally identifiable info that could be stolen. Also, be aware of marketing agreements that allow promotional partners of the budgeting apps to contact you via email and phone. Privacy policies may let you opt out of promotional offers, but please read the fine print.

Budgets are a series of trade-offs. If you spend more in one category, you need to spend less in another. You can direct more money to categories that are meaningful to you personally and cut back in areas that your family won't miss as much.

Budgets represent freedom. Each dollar has a purpose, and you get to decide how to allocate it. You become very intentional about where your money is going.

Some of my clients are well on their way to financial freedom at a young age, and they still prudently track income and spending through a budget. What's holding you back?

Chapter Five

Prepare for Opportunities, Not Just Emergencies

Are you familiar with Maslow's hierarchy of needs[1]? There are basic physiological and safety needs for survival at the base of the pyramid such as food, water, warmth, rest, and security. Once these basic needs are met, you can move to the middle of the pyramid: Belongingness and esteem. These psychological needs include intimate

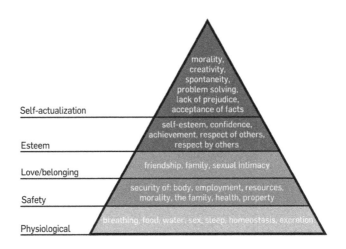

relationships and feelings of accomplishment. At the top of Maslow's pyramid are self-fulfillment needs, focused on achieving your potential.

Maintaining an emergency fund of a few thousand dollars for true emergencies is great because it satisfies basic physiological and safety needs. Unanticipated events can and do happen. Your car breaks down or furnace stops working in the dead of winter. Relying entirely on debt to purchase a new car or furnace is a slippery slope. Tapping into an emergency fund to repair the problem is extremely helpful. Within Maslow's hierarchy, you're maintaining an emergency fund to satisfy basic needs.

Relying on an Emergency Fund for Unemployment

It was devastating to our family when my husband Bryan lost his job in the summer of 2016. It was a shock to both of us! He was fortunate to have a severance package, but that only covered a few months of unemployment. Fortunately, he found a new position before the severance package was depleted. We were grateful that we didn't have to draw on the *emergency* fund. I use the term "emergency fund" because both Bryan and I were then operating under a scarcity mindset, trying to cover our basic needs.

Bryan is a highly educated, hardworking, and ethical man. He attended college on a full-ride scholarship and graduated with undergraduate and graduate accounting degrees in four years. He even earned his MBA in 2013 while working full time. Bryan is an outgoing, charismatic "people-person" as well. He easily strikes up conversations with strangers and makes each child on his team feel special when coaching baseball or soccer. Unemployment wasn't even on our radar in 2016, and having access to an emergency fund was incredibly helpful for our family.

Mindset Change

This book isn't about mere survival—I want to see you and your family thrive! That entails a change of perspective: A shift from scarcity to an abundance, as outlined in Chapter 2. To recap, Steven Covey's 1989 bestseller, *The Seven Habits of Highly Effective People*[2], coined the term "abundance mentality." An abundance mindset helps you:

- Create meaningful life experiences
- Pursue new, interesting opportunities
- Live a full and satisfying life
- Find happiness even amid struggle
- Feel inspired and creative

True transformation requires an abundance mindset. If you foster an abundance mentality, you see the potential to move beyond present circumstances and hope for a brighter future. By contrast, a person operating under the scarcity mindset is consistently concerned that there will never be enough and typically feels like a victim. Emotionally, an abundance mindset makes you feel empowered and engaged, while a scarcity mindset causes frustration and feelings of insecurity.

Let's move up Maslow's hierarchy of needs to belongingness, esteem, and self-actualization. Here, you're focused on intimate relationships, accomplishments, and fulfilling your potential. You are now ready to build an opportunity fund. Saving for the future will seem far more enjoyable.

Imagine this. You've read all the headlines about artificial intelligence and the threat of robots replacing human jobs. The large corporation for which you're working is struggling in today's economic environment. They begin offering early retirement packages to longtime, seasoned employees. That's not enough. Bit by bit, one person per department is losing his or her job. When your boss asks to see you, you have an awful feeling in your gut. Your intuition is right; you are offered a generous six-month severance package in exchange for leaving the company quietly and without any legal action.

At first, you may be in disbelief and don't understand how this happened. You were punctual, had a good rapport with coworkers and a can-do attitude. After the initial shock wears off, this is a perfect time to reflect on the things that really matter in life. Is there a different career that better suits your strengths? Do you need additional schooling to prepare for that career change? Or do you have an entrepreneurial itch to scratch? A business idea may have been on your mind for months or years.

An opportunity fund enables you to slowly build that business, return to school for new career training, or interview for positions in other fields. It gives you time, space, and money to design the professional life you desire.

Let's take another unexpected occurrence: You and your spouse have been trying to conceive for years. Struggles with infertility create emotional scars. You are contemplating adoption or in vitro fertilization. Finally, you become pregnant! The joy you feel for that growing baby cannot be measured.

Then, reality sets in. You begin to think about extra expenses associated with the baby's arrival, such as nursery furniture, a car seat, stroller, diapers, and childcare. Luckily, you and your spouse have been intentional about each dollar saved, and you are ready to draw on the opportunity fund. Shifting to a new normal takes time, and you may not have a great idea of expenses post-baby. The opportunity fund provides peace of mind: you can focus on giving your baby the best possible life.

Now, for a final example. If your home's air conditioner, furnace, or roof is nearing the end of its useful life, draw on your opportunity fund to upgrade to a new one. Systems collapse over time, and it is your responsibility as a homeowner to monitor them. Reinvesting in a new air conditioner, furnace, or roof not only fixes the problem but also may improve energy efficiency. Furthermore, home improvements are aptly named and not confined to large systems that cost thousands of dollars. After 10 years in a home, you may want to upgrade the floors, finish the basement, or install granite countertops in the kitchen. An opportunity fund alleviates financial stress associated with home improvement projects.

Having an opportunity fund means you are operating from an abundance, rather than scarcity, mindset. What if, instead of dwelling on the negative, you begin to see limitless possibilities?

Using an Opportunity Fund for Extended Travel

In 2017, our family had another difficult year. Bryan worked long hours, came home exhausted, and seldom exercised. He rarely had anything to say when I asked about his day. Emotionally and physically, it was apparent that the stress of this job was wearing him down. Our family life suffered as we constantly hurried from one activity to another. We were financially strong, but I was crumbling on the inside. Something had to change.

Seventeen years after my study abroad experience in Madrid, my wish finally came true. Bryan and I decided to take our three boys to Spain for three months. In 2018, we traveled to Barcelona, Valencia, Madrid, and Seville. It was wonderful to witness the beauty and magnificence of these historic cities.

As an entrepreneur who leverages technology to serve clients locally and remotely, I was able to work from my laptop while overseas. Bryan's position, on the other hand, couldn't be handled remotely. Bryan left his corporate treasury role in December 2017, promising me that he would use time in Spain to reevaluate his career. He also agreed to be the primary caretaker for our sons and homeschool them while living in Spain.

We heavily relied on the opportunity fund while living overseas and again when we returned to the US in April. Bryan's search for employment continued over the summer, and childcare and camp expenses were hard to fund on my income alone.

The opportunity fund was valuable because it: 1) enabled us to live in Spain, and 2) provided financial security during Bryan's subsequent job search.

Bryan found new employment in August 2018. Faith in God's plan and an opportunity fund made it happen!

> Career choice matters. Just because you start down one path does not mean you cannot change it a few years later.

Are You Engaged?

Career fit and on-the-job engagement are interconnected. Gallup's "State of the American Workplace"[3] report released in February 2017 found that only 33 percent of US employees were engaged in their jobs. That meant 67 percent were disengaged. **Are you in that 67 percent?**

Being professionally engaged means you have purpose to your work life. Setting and achieving big goals is realistic. Because you are in a state of flow, it doesn't feel like you are "working" most of the time.

If you are lazy or apathetic at work, you probably fall into that 67 percent group and should think about selecting a different career path while building an opportunity fund. Also consider talking to managers who may be able to assign tasks that play to your strengths. Leaving the organization altogether is not the only solution since you may be able to switch roles.

When your personality traits, values, and job responsibilities are in alignment, you are more likely to be engaged at work and it is easier to increase your income. Work satisfaction also spills into other areas of your life. You become a better parent, spouse, sibling, son or daughter, friend, and neighbor.

In other words, career choice matters. Just because you start down one path does not mean you cannot change it a few years later. This concept of job satisfaction is closely tied to an abundance mindset. As Henry Ford once said,

> *"Whether you think you can, or you think you can't—you're right."*

Guidelines for Building an Opportunity Fund

With the right mentality and level of excitement, you can get started on saving for an opportunity fund. Below are three simple steps to build an opportunity fund from scratch:

1. **Start.** Start small, if necessary. After all, Rome wasn't built in a day. Launch the account with $100 if that is all you can spare.
2. **Steadily add cash.** You already accomplished the first step. Now build on that momentum.
3. **Finish.** Get to a point where you feel comfortable with the amount you have saved. Pat yourself on the back for a job well done!

Let's break apart each of these steps into greater detail.

1. START

For step one, consider using an online bank. You can set up a recurring transfer from your checking account, or your employer may allow you to direct deposit a portion of your paycheck into this account. Some clients prefer to establish the account through a bank they do not normally use so it is out of sight and out of mind. Ally Bank, for example, is online only and offers substantially higher interest rates on savings accounts than traditional brick and mortar banks. Other clients think it is simpler to have all family accounts at a single brick and mortar bank for monitoring purposes. If you go this route, recognize that you may sacrifice extra cash since the interest rates for traditional banks are lower than most online only banks.

2. STEADILY ADD CASH

Step two is a little more complicated. There is no magic number for an opportunity fund total because each person's dreams are different. If you want to start a capital-intensive business before transitioning from employee to owner, you will need more money than someone actively engaged in her current profession who has no interest in changing careers nor taking a sabbatical. Furthermore, homeowners should set aside more money than renters for expensive home repairs and improvement projects.

Traditionally, advisors recommend an emergency fund equal to three to 12 months of living expenses. This is a wide range that considers historical expenses. For self-employed people or sole income earners, you are told to err on the side of caution and save a year's worth of living expenses. I recommend that you maintain a small emergency fund for true emergencies and earmark an opportunity fund for higher-level aspirations.

Living purposefully means you are intentional and proactive. An opportunity fund is future oriented. Before you actually need it, get quotes for repairing the roof, A/C unit, furnace, etc. and know each unit's estimated useful life. Research start up business costs and basic personal living expenses if you are an aspiring entrepreneur. Consider the cost of a college education to pursue the profession your heart truly desires. If extended travel is your goal, go online and use free cost-of-living calculators to get a general sense of living expenses in a particular area. Investigate transportation costs such as plane and train tickets or fuel costs if you plan to drive. Do your homework now, and it will save you worry down the road.

Once you have decided on a particular savings target, automate it. It is simple for 401(k) plan participants to increase their contributions by one percent or more each year. You may not have the same option in a traditional savings account, but you *can* set calendar reminders to review progress each quarter and increase your opportunity fund contribution. As discussed in step one, online banks can be really helpful during this step. With the click of a button, you are able to make quick adjustments to the contribution amount.

3. FINISH

This may be the hardest of all the steps. Jon Acuff's book, *Finish*[4], argues that perfectionism is our biggest stumbling block to completing a task, and I agree with Acuff. Perfectionism shows up the day after we start and stays until the end, creating one obstacle after another.

One way to combat perfectionism is to make the goal fun. You have already mentally prepared yourself by repositioning to an abundance mindset. Next, come up with creative ways to stay motivated and accountable while you build an

Prepare for Opportunities, Not Just Emergencies

opportunity fund. If the goal seems impossible, think about cutting it in half or postponing the target completion date. Laser focus on this goal and you will be well on your way to accomplishing it.

Michael Hyatt's book, *Your Best Year Ever*[5], offers additional tactics to achieve goals. Hyatt urges us to consider the "why" behind the goal, connecting with an original motivation. Next, identify potential stumbling blocks and design a strategy to counteract them even before they become an issue. Track progress along the way and see if any modifications are necessary.

Your opportunity fund goal will look different than mine, and that is OK. If you are married, be sure to discuss this with your spouse and get his or her buy-in. It is alright if your spouse isn't as passionate about financial well-being. Nevertheless, ensure you both are heading in the same direction.

Did you ever watch *Tom and Jerry* as a kid? As soon as one gets ahead, the other is pushing him down. You and your spouse should strive to be the opposite of Tom and Jerry. You want to encourage and support each other when obstacles appear.

If you're single, find an accountability partner. He or she will regularly check on your progress and ask what happened if you didn't meet your mini-goal. Reciprocate and offer to be an accountability partner to the other person, too, though it needn't be financial. She/he may have a weight loss goal or may want to improve a relationship with a family member.

The only person separating you from your opportunity fund is you! What are you waiting for?

Chapter Six

Not All Debt is Evil

Steven dreams of leaving his big-time corporate job to live in a remote cabin in a mountainside village. He and his wife, Carol, earn more than $200,000 annually in a city known for its low cost of living. In a word, what is holding them back from fulfilling this dream?

Debt.

Amanda was a straight-A student in high school and earned a spot in a prestigious Pre-Law Scholars program. But her first year in college, she fell into the wrong crowd. Amanda's friends partied hard and spent money frivolously. Well into her thirties, Amanda is still paying off credit card bills from her undergraduate years. Her parents paid for all of her college tuition. What's preventing her from living the carefree lifestyle she envisioned in high school?

Debt.

We live in a materialistic culture where consumerism is glorified. Social media feeds show the highlights of friends' elaborate vacations and second homes. Jealousy ensues. From the time we are babies, we are conditioned to want more: A better life. A happier childhood for our kids.

Our quest for more is toxic. It's OK to seek happiness, but happiness doesn't lie in our material possessions.

Here's a moment of truth, and I want you to be honest with yourself about the answer. Have you ever purchased something because you thought it would make you happy?

I have. You and I make a thousand decisions daily about what to wear, do, and buy. We buy donuts because of their taste, and that temporary happiness in our taste buds means more to us in that moment than the satisfaction of choosing a healthy breakfast.

Our quest for more is toxic. It's OK to seek happiness, but happiness doesn't lie in our material possessions.

We buy clothes or accessories because they make us feel good; we're happy when someone compliments us. We buy luxury cars because they define social status.

I'll let you in on a little secret. **Most millionaires don't buy luxury cars.** If they do, they conduct ample research and buy *used* luxury cars.

Spending money on things that bring you or your family happiness isn't inherently bad. Those purchases become burdens when you spend money you don't have, with no plan to pay off that debt.

Not all debt is evil. But most of it is. Let's sort through some of the basics.

Good, or Acceptable, Debt

If you're like most people, it seems downright impossible to pay for a house with cash. Instead, you rely on a mortgage to finance most of the home purchase. I'd strongly urge you to save at least 20 percent of the home's purchase price for a down payment, whether you are a first-time homebuyer or not. Otherwise, you will have to take out a secondary loan or pay Private Mortgage Insurance.

What if the value of your home declines after the initial purchase? That happened to me in 2005 near the peak of the US real estate market. I wasn't a financial advisor then and had only saved 10 percent for the down payment. My first home was a big financial mistake—at least a $15,000 loss on a $150,000 home when you factor in closing costs, realtor commissions, and renovations.

However, mortgage debt can be good. Now, my husband Bryan and I live in a nice suburban home with at least 40 percent in home equity. We secured a 3.5 percent interest rate for a fixed 30-year mortgage when refinancing in 2013 and interest rates were at historic lows. We could have chosen a 15-year fixed mortgage but opted for a 30-year term to provide greater cash flow flexibility. We refinanced when I was preparing to leave my job and knew we would live off one income for a while. The monthly payment on a 15-year mortgage would have been too much for us to handle. In higher income years, Bryan and I have the option of prepaying the mortgage and applying additional payments to principal.

One other historic advantage of a mortgage was its tax deductibility. Prior to 2018, this was a huge benefit for families who owned a single home. Given the US tax law changes at the end of 2017, which are not expected to sunset until 2025, more families will be taking the standard deduction than ever before. Even if you itemized deductions in the past, it may be more advantageous in 2018 and beyond to take the enhanced standard deduction. Mortgage interest will be deductible, up to certain limits, if you still plan to itemize deductions.

Paying off a mortgage ahead of schedule feels good emotionally. The peace of mind associated with an early payoff may more than justify any financial tradeoff. Financially speaking, however, you may be doing yourself a disservice by prepaying the mortgage. Interest rates should be factored into any decision to prepay the mortgage. Suppose you inherit $100,000 and your mortgage balance is $100,000. If you invest the inheritance in a taxable brokerage account and expect to earn 6 percent return on that investment, it makes more sense to invest rather than pay down a 3.5 percent mortgage.

Similarly, when you have just a few years remaining on your mortgage and most of the monthly payment is applied to principal rather than interest, it makes financial sense to continue with the mortgage payment so long as your interest rate is relatively low. Some of my former clients with excess cash opted to keep the mortgage simply because of the mortgage interest deduction and interest rate differential.

Student loans are another type of acceptable debt when used wisely. In many cases, undergraduate degrees are required to get into any white-collar position. Some professions demand additional schooling. A newly-minted doctor could easily have more than $200,000 in student loan debt but also has higher anticipated earnings.

The type of position someone plans to pursue after college dictates their recommended maximum of amount of student loans. For example, a teacher whose starting salary is $30,000 shouldn't take out more than $30,000 in undergraduate student loans.

Federal Direct Loans[1] offer competitive interest rates. Students with demonstrated financial need can take subsidized loans, and the federal government pays interest on the loans while the student is in school with a six-month grace period thereafter. Unsubsidized Federal Direct Loans are available to all students who complete the FAFSA, regardless of financial need, but interest accrues while in school. Presently, dependent students may take a maximum of $31,000 in federal loans, of which $23,000 can be subsidized[2]. Independent graduate or professional students have much higher federal loan limits.

Is your child going to college soon? If the answer is yes, have a candid conversation with him or her about creating a debt pay-off plan. Think about their chosen career field, average annual earnings and time it takes to secure a position. Is your child entering an industry where supply outweighs demand? Some advanced degrees no longer carry as much weight. I know a handful of law school graduates who could not find reasonable employment within a year of graduation, let alone a six-figure salary with a top-tier firm.

Consider your future earnings and available financial resources if you are a student or will soon be pursuing an advanced degree. If paying for college with cash will prevent you from paying your credit card bill, take the student loan since it probably has a lower interest rate than the credit card.

Whether it is mortgage or student loan debt, remember the virtue of prudence. Proceed with caution and ensure there is enough wiggle room in your current or future budget to make consistent payments. Just because you're approved for a sizable mortgage doesn't mean you should take it. Similarly, once you've maxed out Federal Direct Loans, don't pursue private loans unless you have a clear plan to eradicate them after graduation.

Bad Debt

Unlike acceptable forms of debt, such as mortgage and student loans, most debt can be crippling. Credit card companies prey on people who make minimum payments. This may sound harsh, but it's true: **Only buy on credit if you can pay off the balance in full each month**. Making the minimum payments exacerbates the issue because you will accrue mounds of interest expense.

Credit cards are not the only type of debt. Car sales are at an all-time high. If you are concerned with what friends and neighbors are driving, you may be tempted to buy a new car every few years and fully finance its cost.

This is a dangerous.

The desire to "Keep Up with the Jones" really impacts your ability to build long-term wealth. When does it stop? After you have a luxury car? Two of them?

A car depreciates quickly. If you purchase one for $35,000[3], it may only be worth $30,000 a year later. Not only are you making monthly payments but you're also going to get far less money when you sell it. Additionally, there is no tax deduction for personal vehicle financing. The solution is to hold on to your car *at least* seven years. Save up for the next car when you do not have any more payments on your current vehicle.

Houston, We've Got a Problem

Living paycheck-to-paycheck is a common reality for many Americans. We buy, buy, buy instead of creating and adhering to a budget. This leads to short-term thinking. Rather, we should be focused on long-term goals like financial independence.

How do you know when you're in over your head? If you're spending what you are earning (or more) with no room for savings, you need to find a way to move away from short-term thinking and define a long-term plan.

Several financial bloggers write about how they didn't have a background in personal finance. Instead, they realized their financial path was a destructive one, redefined values and goals, and aggressively pursued those goals.

Nicole Rule of *greatestworth.com* and her husband, Sam, started their $100,000 debt pay-off journey when she was pregnant with their second child. Seeing their negative net financial worth statement got them out of the consumerist trap and helped them stick with a budget. They gave up every "luxury" for 26 months, including vacations, dining out, gym memberships, cable TV, and baby music classes. Nicole sacrificed so she could be a stay-at-home mother, full of freedom and opportunity.

Financial problems and debt-related stress, in particular, wreak havoc on many marriages. Brett Oblack of *Step*

1 Minimalist[4] describes five ways that minimalism has strengthened his marriage:

1. Better financial control
2. Honest communication
3. Less stressful and expensive holidays
4. Better health
5. Support for passion and values

Joshua Becker, author of *Wall Street Journal* bestseller, *The More of Less*, is well known for tendencies towards minimalism. One spring morning in 2008, Joshua and his five-year-old son were cleaning the garage while neighbors tended to the garden. The neighbor said something that struck a chord in Joshua, "The more stuff you own, the more your stuff owns you."

Becoming a minimalist hasn't simply affected the finances of Joshua's family. He admits that it is a spiritual journey as well, writing that "now it's about living a life that is honoring the God who created me."

Some people pursue a minimalist lifestyle strictly because of the financial freedom it provides. Fewer things, less clutter, more money in your pocket. You can sell or donate items that no longer hold value to you. Other people pursue minimalism when they wake up to the excess and realize that material possessions cannot fill the void in their lives.

I fall in the second camp. I'm fascinated by minimalism and want to explore it further (if I can get my husband Bryan on board).

If you are part of the first group and want to embark on a minimalist lifestyle, power to you! Pursuing it will help you climb out of debt even faster.

Pay Down Debt or Save?

Of course, it's not always that easy. How do you know when to pay down debt versus save more for retirement? Apply these principles in order:

1. BUILD EMERGENCY AND OPPORTUNITY FUNDS

As discussed in Chapter 5, an emergency fund provides a financial cushion for unexpected events and is necessary for survival. When you are ready to move up Maslow's hierarchy to psychological and self-fulfillment needs, you're at a different level. It becomes far easier to have an abundance mindset and build an opportunity fund. An opportunity fund allows you to start a new business, travel more, complete home renovations, or accomplish other goals.

2. GET THE EMPLOYER MATCH

Ensure you are contributing enough to your employer's retirement plan to take full advantage of the company match. It's essentially free money.

3. WEIGH THE INVESTMENT RATE OF RETURN VS. DEBT INTEREST RATE

Let's assume you have already built a small emergency fund and are taking advantage of your employer's retirement plan match. Let's further suppose that you have a $10,000 credit card balance on which you pay nondeductible interest of 15 percent. By getting rid of those interest payments, you're effectively getting a 15 percent return on your money! Which sounds better, paying off this credit card or earning 7 percent in an investment account? Eliminating high interest debt is a bigger priority.

4. CONSIDER A HYBRID APPROACH

If you are an intensely focused person who values logic over emotion, making the best financial decision gives you satisfaction. Emotion may not come into the equation. You focus all energy on paying down "bad" debt.

For others, financial and emotional decisions function differently. What makes the most financial sense may not "feel" good. You may have multiple goals, such as paying down student loan debt, saving for retirement, and funding your child's education. Dedicating all of your financial resources toward a single goal might not make sense to you. Instead, allocate a small amount of money toward each goal.

Debt, when used properly, can be a great tool to achieve your financial goals. But debt also can negatively impact your financial future if you do not use it responsibly.

Credit Scores

There is a lot of confusion surrounding credit scores, and there are different schools of thought on whether you even need a credit score. Some personal finance books make you feel guilty for taking on any kind of debt (including a mortgage). They contend credit scores are unnecessary, even when purchasing a home or car. There are very few mortgage brokers who will offer a mortgage when you do not have a credit history. If you happen to stumble upon such a lender, the interest rate he or she offers will likely be higher than current market rates because they consider you a "gamble." Furthermore, no credit history may make it difficult to rent in the nicer parts of town.

Credit scores are based on a couple of factors:

1. **Payment history:**
Your track record matters. Payment history is the most important factor and accounts for 35 percent of your credit score. Pay your bills on time and in full. Late charges and delinquencies create red flags on your credit report. Recurring, automatic payments are wonderful for this reason. You can set them and forget them as long as your payment information doesn't change.

2. **Ratio of debt to overall credit line:**
Many people think you should use all available credit, but that's wrong. The utilization ratio looks at the amount of available credit compared to the amount you actually use. Aim for a low utilization ratio, ideally 30 percent or less. For example, if you are approved for $1,000 a month, charge a maximum of $300 on that credit card monthly and pay it off in full. Lenders consider borrowers who max out their credit to be people who cannot handle their debt responsibly. The total outstanding debt accounts for 30 percent of your credit score.

3. **Length of credit history:**
If you are in your forties and have been responsibly using credit for more than 20 years, you have an advantage over a 22-year-old college graduate applying for his first credit card.

Also, consider leaving inactive credit cards open. Whether it was a substantial home improvement purchase at Home Depot or a shopping spree at Banana Republic, you may have opened a store-specific credit card years ago and find you no longer shop there. The balance was paid in full and you haven't charged anything on the card for months. Rather than closing the account, inquire about the inactive policy. Length of credit history represents 15 percent of your total credit score.

4. Credit mix and new credit:

Repaying a mix of revolving credit and installment loans show that you are responsible and trustworthy when it comes to managing credit. There is too much of a good thing, though. Opening several credit lines simultaneously may show the lender you are in financial trouble. Credit mix and new credit each account for 10 percent of your total credit score.

Don't fall into the trap of having multiple credit card accounts with outstanding balances and no plan to pay them. It's a downward spiral that impacts your likelihood of paying the balances on time while maintaining low utilization ratios.

Big Spender

As you probably know, marriage is a lot of give and take. Compromise is essential. But I've witnessed too many instances where a husband or wife has a spending problem. It leads to financial concerns and puts severe emotional strain on the relationship. If you find yourself in this situation, here are some tips you may find helpful.

Set some ground rules together. Jointly decide on a dollar amount that must be "approved" by the other spouse before being spent. Obviously, you will consult your spouse on large purchases like cars or homes. You don't need to micromanage gas tank refills or grocery expenditures. What about other items in the gray area? If your spouse wants to buy a guitar or piece of exercise equipment on Home Shopping Network, should he consult you?

I bring up these examples because my husband, Bryan, made both of these purchases within the last 10 years. We had no ground rules at the time and quickly realized that was a mistake. Now, we discuss any extraordinary purchase beyond $100. A grocery bill that exceeds $100 doesn't matter, but a musical instrument purchase merits further discussion.

Maybe your ground rules are structured around the type of expenditure rather than a specific dollar threshold. Perhaps you can agree to check with each other first on any "nontraditional" purchases, such as home furnishings and lawncare products.

Some couples think they can skip this step by simply having separate accounts. I don't think this solves the problem. There is an underlying issue and separate accounts only exacerbate it. I'm a big proponent of joint accounts because they have built-in accountability. When the Bible says, "the two shall become one," we should listen. The sacrament of marriage is carefully intertwined into our daily lives, and finances are a big component.

On a related note, it is important to jointly create a budget and regularly check-in with each other. Honesty and transparency are critical in your marriage. That includes financial transparency.

You don't have to carry the burden alone. Be honest with yourself and your spouse about struggles to adhere to a budget. Opposites often attract. Your spouse may be able to offer suggestions on how to say "no" to a tempting yet unnecessary purchase. Keeping lines of communication open likely strengthens your marriage.

A Success Story

One of my client couples, Eli and Christina, started working with me in January 2017. Eli had about $480,000 of financial net worth and Christina had negative $25,000—primarily from student loans at rates of 6.8 percent and above. They set an initial goal to eradicate more than $120,000 of Christina's student loans within five years.

When discussing cash flow, I discovered that Eli and Christina were spending approximately $15,000 annually on personal training expenses. Christina became pregnant with their first child, and that $15,000 is now used for daycare expenses. Eli and Christina stopped using separate accounts and hyper-focused on Christina's goal of paying down student loan debt.

We refinanced their mortgage to free up cash, and Christina put $4,000 monthly toward student loan payments. This allowed her to accomplish the goal in half the time. Eli and Christina's combined financial net worth has increased by more than $200,000 in under two years.

Their marriage is stronger than ever. There's no resentment from Eli because he was fortunate to come into the marriage with no student loan debt and wanted to support Christina's goal. Now that they are free of student debt, extra cash flow goes towards the baby's college fund and their investment portfolio.

I love this story because it illustrates how spouses working toward a common goal are stronger together. Christina earns more than Eli and wants to step back to an 80 percent reduced workload, so Eli is increasing his workload responsibility and pay. Their combined income will remain the same. Eli doesn't mind putting his earnings toward Christina's debt payments because it lays a better foundation for their long-term goals of financial independence and college funding.

Eli and Christina aren't the only ones working toward a debt-free lifestyle. What is holding you back from being the next success story?

Chapter Seven

Value-Based Investing Works

I used to believe investing was separate from financial planning, that they were these two distinct items and never overlapped. Why do we create boundaries?

Real financial planning (and investing) happens where money and values intersect.

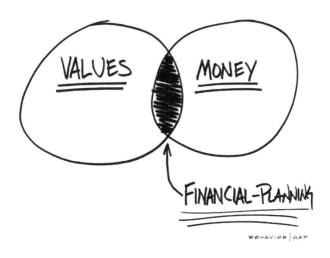

My first experience with investing started in 1999. I was intrigued by an introductory high school economics class. Our teacher, Mrs. Weiss, challenged us to create a test portfolio with five individual equities and track their performance throughout the semester.

The tech industry was booming at the time. Cisco, Hewlett Packard, and a few other stocks rounded out my portfolio. But I didn't stop at the hypothetical portfolio. I invested $2,000 of my hard-earned dollars from part-time jobs into these companies. My $2,000 investment declined to $1,000 within a few months. Emotionally, I was a wreck and ended up selling the positions for $1,000—a 50 percent decline from the purchase price.

I felt like a failure. How could I be duped into buying high and selling low? There were a few reasons for this setback:

1. **Naivety.** It was my first time investing in the stock market. Had I been a more seasoned investor, I may have recognized the tech "bubble." What goes up must eventually come down, right?
2. **Lack of diversification.** Mrs. Weiss explained the dangers of putting all your metaphorical eggs into one basket. I believe only one of my five holdings was outside the tech industry.
3. **Emotional decision making.** We all *want* to make rational choices. Yet in reality, many of us make decisions guided by our emotions. I'm a heart-centered person. If something doesn't feel right in my gut, I explore ways to make a change. On the other hand, my husband, Bryan, is a very rational decision maker. He is a great sounding board for any big decisions. Fortunately, that early investing

mistake also helped me become a rational investor. I didn't sell any equity positions during the last recession.

My Investment Philosophy

Failures are prerequisites to growth. That early experience certainly shaped my investment philosophy today. Remember:

1. Start with the big picture plan and decide if your investments fit that plan.
2. Don't try to "time" the market.
3. Stock-picking is a gamble.
4. Take an academic, research-tested approach to investing.
5. Do not let the tax tail wag the dog.
6. Consider your investment portfolio for charitable giving.
7. Beware of hidden fees.
8. Rationality wins.

I. Get Clear on Your Why

Think back to the questions posed in Chapters 1, 2, and 3. Why do you do what you do? How are you called to be a better version of yourself? What does your ideal life look like? Where do you want to be five years from now?

Begin with this overarching vision, and then design multiple goals around that vision. Figure out *why* you want to reach financial independence earlier than the traditional age of 65 and what steps you need to take to get there. Your retirement goal is heavily influenced by the investment mix or asset allocation. Age doesn't matter as much. If you are within five years of being financially independent and will be drawing down your investment portfolio to fund this lifestyle, your asset mix should be more conservative than someone who is 20 years away from financial independence.

That is why I don't like target date retirement funds. They assume all 30-year-olds are 35 years away from retirement. And that simply isn't the case anymore. Equally, they assume all 65-year-olds will retire this year. Some people prefer to work into their seventies and will want a more aggressive asset mix.

One of my client couples is within five years of financial independence. Tom and Sally have about 80 percent of their investment portfolio in equities and the other 20 percent in fixed income and cash. They will heavily rely on a taxable investment account to fund their family's lifestyle costs for at least 15 years. I advised them in mid-2018 to reposition about 10 percent of their taxable account balance from equities to municipal bonds. Having an equity-heavy portfolio is great when the stock market is rising but can be disastrous when the market is declining. Rebounding takes a much longer time, and time is not on their side if they want to retire within five years.

Take a hard look at your investment portfolio. Do your current investments align with your goals?

Give thought to each account and its purpose. Retirement accounts such as 401(k) plans, 403(b) plans, and IRAs often are earmarked for retirement. What about 529 college saving plans? Is the investment mix in your 529 plan too conservative or aggressive for the estimated drawdown date? Are you keeping your opportunity fund in cash or choosing long-term investments that could fluctuate in value?

Consistency is key when matching an account's investment mix with its intended goal. For any mismatch, find a tax-efficient way to get rid of the position. In a tax-sheltered retirement or 529 plan account, there is no tax consequence for selling. But you need to exercise caution with taxable brokerage accounts. Carefully calculate the tax implications (federal and state) if you want to dispose of an appreciated position in your brokerage account where the current value is much higher than the cost basis (i.e. $1,000 FMV and $400 basis = $600 gain). It may be wiser to choose a different position where the value and basis are closer (e.g. $1,000 FMV and $800 basis = $200 gain).

To reiterate, start with the big picture plan and decide if your investments fit that plan.

II. Beware of Market Timing

Do you remember having a Magic 8-Ball when you were a kid? You would ask a question, shake the ball, and turn it over for an answer. I've always been a curious person and would often repeat the question to see if the ball produced the same answers. I discovered I shouldn't put too much stock into the answers spewing from a $10 toy.

When you try to time the market, it's as if you are putting your investment portfolio into the hands of the Magic 8-Ball.

You tactically move in and out of positions based on whether you think the stock market will go up or down on a given day. Market timing is more than a gamble. It's downright exhausting.

Instead, develop a long-term asset mix and stick to it. Assess the level of risk you are willing to take in your investment portfolio and see if your existing assets reflect that risk. Think about the last market downturn. Did you check your retirement account balances every day even though you were five years or more from financial independence? If the answer is yes, you may want to consider a conservative portfolio. If you looked at retirement account balances only to buy additional assets during the last downturn, an aggressive investment mix may be better for you.

When defining an ideal portfolio mix, remember that market cycles are normal. Prior to the fall of 2018, we were in the longest US bull market run in history. The S&P 500 reached record highs. By the time this book is published, we could be in a deep recession. There is no Magic 8-Ball to tell us when the next downturn will happen. There are indicators, but economists rarely predict *every* market downturn.

Also remember only 10 percent of your investment performance is attributable to the positions you choose. The other 90 percent of performance is based on the asset mix, or ratio of stocks to bonds. You may want a single investment strategy for all accounts. Or, it may be easier to develop two strategies—one that is short-term and another that is focused more on long-term goals.

Never try to time the market.

III. Blackjack, Anyone?

Similar to market timing, individual stock selection is a gamble. There are fundamentals you can study, but the time and energy you have to devote to it is probably better spent with family and friends. For nonprofessionals, luck is the biggest component. Additionally, stock picking can quickly become addictive. Like a shopaholic who feels a surge of dopamine after every purchase, a stock picker experiences a similar mental boost when his stock reaches a new level. The opposite holds true, too. When a shopaholic finds her credit cards are frozen or a stock picker sees a 10 percent decline in stock price one day, the pain is real. It's tempting for a stock picker to buy and sell multiple times a week to maximize gains or minimize losses. When does it stop?

An investor focused on long-term goals has a much easier time handling any daily stock market fluctuations. When it comes to investing, are you preparing for a sprint or marathon? If Aesop's fable, *The Tortoise and the Hare*, is any indication, slow and steady often wins the race.

IV. It's Hard to Find Unicorns

When you hear the word unicorn, what comes to mind? I picture the mystical creatures I dreamt about as a little girl. Among tech start-ups, unicorns refer to companies with a one-billion-dollar valuation or more.

In the investing world, think about unicorns in the context of Uber, Tesla, and Apple. Trying to find the next unicorn is like searching for a needle in a haystack.

Instead of focusing on individual stocks (or unicorns), look at buying a basket of companies. Mutual funds and exchange traded funds, or ETFs, offer the benefits of diversification. For instance, Vanguard Total Stock Market ETF invests its portfolio across market capitalization (large, mid, and small cap stocks) as well as style (growth and value). Growth-oriented companies tend to reinvest their earnings in innovative projects while value-oriented companies usually return their profits to shareholders in the form of dividends.

Some mutual funds are active in nature, while others are passive. Active managers try to select stocks that will outperform their peers and charge a hefty premium to do it. The manager may have started as a stock analyst and earned his or her Chartered Financial Analyst designation before climbing the corporate ladder. Passive funds, on the other hand, invest in a broad basket of stocks within a particular sector that are unlikely to "beat" the market. Because passive funds often buy and hold positions, they are inexpensive compared to their active peers.

According to CNBC[1], only 10 percent of large-cap active managers consistently outperform their benchmark over a 15-year time span. *Even for mutual fund managers who make their living analyzing stocks, only 10 percent of them are able to beat the market time and time again.*

Taking a research-based approach to investing means you invest in mutual funds and exchange traded funds that fine tune their method of capturing returns. These fund managers strike a nice balance between costs to the investor and expected returns.

Companies like Vanguard managed more than five trillion dollars of assets in January 2018 because people recognized that passive, low-cost investing works well over the long-term. An academic, research-tested approach to investing is smart.

V. Taxes Are Important but Not Everything

You may find yourself at a crossroads. A position in your investment portfolio isn't performing as well as expected for the fee or perhaps it doesn't fit with your financial goals. If you want to dispose of a position in a taxable account, taxes should be only one consideration.

In the US, you'll pay ordinary income tax rates on short-term gains. However, holding the position a year or more makes it a long-term taxable gain and you'll pay a lower rate. If you are in one of the bottom two US income tax brackets, you may pay **no** federal long-term capital gains tax. The zero percent long-term capital gains tax rate applied to married couples filing jointly with taxable income of $77,200 or less in 2018. Married couples with taxable income between $77,201 and $479,000 only had a 15 percent federal long-term capital gains tax rate in 2018.

Market downturns offer great opportunities to lock in tax losses within taxable brokerage accounts. You can deduct up to $3,000 of net capital losses per tax year, and any excess losses can be carried forward to future tax years.

Net Capital Loss = Total Capital Loss – Total Capital Gain

Let's suppose you have capital losses totaling $10,000 and capital gains totaling $6,000. That is a net capital loss of $4,000. Of that $4,000, you can take a current tax deduction for $3,000 and carry the remaining $1,000 loss to next year's tax return.

Any capital loss or gain within a tax-deferred or tax-protected account does not get reported on your income tax return. You are taxed on 401(k) and traditional IRA withdrawals as you take money out of the account, not as you are rebalancing to new investments.

Don't let the tax tail wag the dog.

VI. Satisfying Philanthropic Goals Through Investments

If you're reading this book, you likely have a philanthropic heart. You want to help others—financially, emotionally, and spiritually. Did you know you can help financially through your investment portfolio?

Positions with high fair market value and low tax basis (also known as highly appreciated positions) in taxable brokerage accounts are ideal for charitable contributions. We'll discuss the strategy in detail in Chapter 10, but understand now that it is a possibility. Cash isn't the only way to support charitable causes.

The strategy also works well for concentrated stock positions from a prior or current employer. If you vest in stock options or receive Restricted Stock Units, a very large portion of your investment portfolio may be tied to your employer. Donating shares of stock to a charity provides several benefits: You support a meaningful cause. You diversify your investment portfolio. And you avoid capital gains tax.

In short, consider your investment portfolio for charitable giving.

VII. Buyer Beware

Do you ever dread buying a new car? I do. Not because I'm unexcited about driving a car but because I think of all those "gotcha" fees that are hidden until you're ready to sign on the dotted line. If I know my car salesman is working on commission, I am leery he may steer me towards a more expensive car solely because it earns him a higher commission. I prefer to buy a vehicle from someone who is transparent about compensation and who receives a flat fee, regardless of whether I drive away in a $20,000 or $50,000 car.

We'll cover this more in Chapter 13, but there are two different types of financial advisors. The vast majority of advisors are affiliated with a broker-dealer. They often earn a commission for each investment that is purchased or sold. Unfortunately, brokers do not have a legal duty to tell you the underlying cost of an investment or disclose their personal compensation. Brokers generally follow a suitability standard, which means they only need to recommend a suitable product or investment position—not necessarily one in the client's best interest.

Independent, fee-only advisors like myself are compensated for the advice we give on a variety of financial topics. A comprehensive financial planner will offer guidance on cash flow management, retirement, college funding, insurance policies, and estate planning. We are 100 percent transparent with fees, so you know exactly how much we will be compensated—from the beginning of the relationship. Fee-only advisors follow the more stringent fiduciary standard, which means our recommendations are always in the client's best interest.

At my investment advisory firm WorthyNest®, we find that inexpensive, passive exchange traded funds are typically the quickest way to build long-term wealth. Our clients are already paying a fee for our expert guidance, and we don't want them to pay additional fees unless it truly adds value.

In short, beware of hidden fees.

VIII. Rational Investors Have It Easier

As I said before, emotions often drive our decision-making as human beings, and that has advantages and disadvantages. Decisions guided by emotion are often reactive. They can be helpful in times of danger or if consequences are minimal. If you drop kids off at school in the morning, your brain may go into autopilot mode until you arrive. Emotions enable you to slam on the brakes if a small child walks across the street in front of your car.

If you are confronted with several logical solutions to a problem, emotions may enable the final selection. However, emotions also may create biases or distort reality.

Fear is a strong emotion felt by many when the stock market is declining. Likewise, euphoria may drive our emotions when the stock market is performing well. Finding a rational compromise between these two extremes is essential to sound investing. If you consider yourself an "emotional" investor, you may find immense value in an investment advisor who can remind you of your overall objectives.

When it comes to investing, rationality wins.

Values-Based Investing

Now that you have an idea of my general investment philosophy, let's discuss how investing actually correlates to values. Socially responsible investing (SRI) is commonly known as socially conscious, ethical, green, or sustainable investing. These strategies emphasize not only financial return but also social or environmental good to instill positive change. SRI funds typically invest in companies on the forefront of environmental stewardship, diversity and inclusion, and human rights. Other SRI funds avoid businesses that sell tobacco, alcohol, weapons, or contraceptives.

Vanguard's FTSE Social Index Fund is an example of a socially responsible fund that invests in large capitalization companies. Its largest holdings are Apple, Microsoft, Facebook, JP Morgan, and Google. Carrying a 0.2 percent management fee, it offers diversification similar to the S&P 500 Index but with a social and environmental filter.

Some firms have taken SRI one step further with biblically responsible investments (BRI). For instance, Inspire invests in biblically aligned companies that create meaningful impact worldwide. Half of Inspire's management fee profits support Christian ministries. I researched BRI funds extensively but have not found any yet that align with my investment philosophy. BRI funds often have higher management fees and shorter track records. Until this trend reverses, I'd rather use socially responsible funds that have been around five years or more and have a management fee of 0.5 percent or less.

At the end of the day, you are in the driver's seat. Researching some SRI funds that screen out "sin stocks" may be a good starting point. Rate performance relative to their benchmarks: compare US large cap blended positions to the S&P 500 Index or international large cap positions to the MSCI EAFE Index. If the management fee is reasonable and you see some performance advantage, consider adding that position to your investment portfolio.

Always remember to keep monitoring it. You may find you only want to place hard-earned dollars into socially responsible investments, or the cost of holding SRI funds may feel greater than the benefits—both financially and psychologically. Or, like me, you may enjoy holding a little of both: Traditional, passive exchange traded funds and a few SRI funds. The choice is yours.

Chapter Eight

Even the Faithful Have Insurance

(But You Can't Emergency-Proof Your Life)

Why have insurance if you are faithful to God the Almighty, Maker of Heaven and Earth? Because insurance isn't about you; it's about your family. Insurance is a means of protecting against loss. All parents should consider life, disability, and health insurance.

Emergencies are inevitable. When you purchase an insurance policy, you're transferring some, but not all, risk from yourself to an outside third party. You agree to pay premiums in exchange for that transfer of risk.

Life Insurance

When you think of insurance, what is the first type to come to mind? It's probably life insurance. You want to protect family members from financial distress when your time on earth is done.

But there is a huge difference between protection and overabundance. Some of my clients push back on life insurance recommendations because they do not want their loved ones to be in a better financial position without them than they are now. For example, suppose you have $500,000 saved and a life insurance policy for $1 million. If you die, your family inherits $1.5 million (savings and life insurance proceeds)—leaving them in a better financial position on the surface. What cannot be ignored, however, is your foregone earnings. If you're in your thirties or forties with a child at home, your future earnings may quickly exceed the value of the life insurance policy. Losing a parent is hard enough emotionally. Don't make a short-sighted decision financially and skimp on insurance.

Identifying the proper amount of life insurance coverage is difficult. On one level, you are covering the costs of final expenses (e.g. funeral and burial), debts (e.g. mortgage and credit cards), and living expenses of surviving family members. On another level, it's important to look at protecting your future earnings. Before we discuss specifics on the amount of coverage, let's focus on three main types of life insurance.

Term Life Insurance

For young families especially, term life insurance is a good choice. It is the most inexpensive type of life insurance policy and akin to renting, rather than buying, a home. You only have coverage if you continue to pay the premiums. Some term life policies have an increasing premium because they assume your earnings will increase. Other term policies are fixed, which means that your premium will remain the same each year for the duration of the policy. Under the fixed policy, premiums are higher the longer the term. For instance, your annual premium may be $1,000 for a 15-year level term but $1,300 for a 20-year level term. Just because you select a longer fixed term doesn't mean you have to continue paying premiums for the duration of the term. But if you elect a shorter level term policy (i.e. 10 years) and want the policy one more year (i.e. year 11), expect your premium to skyrocket the following year.

Large employers often provide basic life insurance coverage equal to one or two times your annual salary at no cost to you. They also may offer supplemental group policies for an additional cost, but the premiums of these group policies vary significantly by employer.

One of my clients is a federal agent. She was paying more than $500 annually for $500,000 of coverage as a government employee. We looked at individual term quotes and found a policy with a slightly lower premium for one million dollars of coverage. She could get double the coverage for less cost by using an outside, individual policy. Her employer penalized young, healthy employees in their group life insurance policy. If she were 20 years older, her employer-provided group policy may have been the better deal.

Whole Life Insurance

Compared to term insurance, whole life policies offer valuable long-term protection. Cash value builds in the policy while you make out-of-pocket premiums. You can take loans against the cash value but should be wary of high interest rates.

Whole life policies are expensive because of the level premiums, fixed death benefit, and other benefits like dividends and loans. You are no longer required to make out-of-pocket premium payments when the whole life policy is "paid up."

When I began working with very affluent families in 2006, I found myself collaborating with insurance agents on whole life policies for clients. Many of these families were using life insurance to pass more wealth to heirs without paying additional taxes. I became engrossed in this world of estate planning and tax mitigation and pursued a whole life policy for myself. In my mid-twenties, my annual premium was $3,000 for $500,000 of death benefit. Much of the premium in the early years was directed towards the agent's commission and internal costs. My policy was left with very little cash value when interest rates took a nosedive. The projected dividends in 2006 were far lower than actual dividends.

About 10 years after starting that policy, I decided it wasn't worth it. My accumulated premium payments were slightly more than the cash value of the policy. I had the option of taking the policy "paid up" and reducing the death benefit to $130,000 *OR* removing the cash value with minimal tax consequence. I choose the latter. Paying off my car loan and purchasing a new $1 million term life policy ($450 annual premium) provided better bang for the buck.

Universal Life Insurance

Whole life insurance is not the only type of permanent policy. Universal life insurance offers flexibility in the premium payment and death benefit. Suppose you start a universal life policy for $3,000 annually and lose your job 10 years into the policy. Check with your insurance agent to see if there is enough cash value in the policy so you don't have to pay the premium out-of-pocket. Then, resume premium payments in the following year when you're in a better financial position.

On the opposite end of the spectrum, assume you have an unexpected financial windfall this year and want to stop paying premiums on the universal life policy in subsequent years. You may pay a lump sum (up to specified policy limits) and drastically decrease or stop paying premiums altogether in later years.

Amount of Coverage

Now that you understand the types of life insurance, let's shift the focus to the proper amount of coverage. Life insurance premiums are more expensive for men than women due to shorter life expectancies.

There used to be a rule of thumb among insurance agents that your death benefit on a term life policy should be your annual pre-tax income, multiplied by seven to 10. For example, if your income is $100,000, you would have $700,000 to $1,000,000 of term life insurance protection. Below are three types of people for whom this rule of thumb is *not* helpful:

I.   Stay-at-home parents:

You are not receiving financial compensation for hard work at home if you are a stay-at-home parent. Following the rule of thumb, you should have no life insurance coverage because your financial earnings are zero. However, your spouse would need to secure childcare and may require other professional services if you prematurely pass away. Examples of these services include housekeeping, laundry, meal delivery, and home maintenance.

Your spouse's salary should be carefully considered. If, for instance, your spouse is a physician, he or she may be able to cover these additional costs with earnings. In this case, focus on adequate life insurance on your spouse's life and protect his or her future earnings.

If you decide it is worthwhile to pursue coverage as a stay-at-home parent, consider the total cost to provide all the services for which you are responsible. Multiply that annual amount by the number of years that your children will require financial support. A stay-at-home parent with two toddlers will likely require more life insurance than a parent with two teenagers who will be out of the house in a few years.

II. Parents with young kids:

Budgeting as a young family is tough. You are steadily building work experience and have the added expenses of childcare and schooling. It is wise to consider MORE than 10 times your salary. Think about future expenses and how long it will take you to amass enough wealth to accommodate your family's needs.

My family has a mortgage, and our three boys are ages four, six, and nine. Childcare and private grade school tuition totals $22,000 annually. My husband and I also plan to send all three boys to Catholic high school, another $15,000 annually per child. That figure is not even factoring in the costs of clothes, activities, and food for our growing boys. College is expensive, and we must consider that as well. After carefully reviewing these expenses and our future earnings, we decided 10 times annual salary is not nearly enough to fund our family's lifestyle. Bryan and I each have coverage closer to 20 times our annual earnings.

III. Persons with substantial assets:

For term life insurance especially, age is not on your side. Premiums increase substantially in your fifties and sixties. If you are within a few years of financial independence and have amassed enough wealth to live comfortably, you may want to consider self-insuring. That means you will use existing assets in lieu of an outside life insurance policy. If, however, you are insistent on having some form of life insurance, consider permanent policies such as whole life or universal life.

Disability Insurance

Life insurance may be an obvious choice to protect your family. What about disability insurance?

> Unfortunately, only 10 percent of individuals accurately estimate their chance of disability.

TMA Insurance Trust shares some startling statistics[1]:
- One in three working Americans will become disabled for 90 days or more before age 65.
- One in eight workers will be disabled for five years or more during their lifetime.
- The average group long-term disability claim lasts 34.6 months.
- Ninety percent of disabilities are caused by illness, not accidents.

Short-term disability policies cover six months of disability or less. I usually recommend building up cash reserves rather than paying a premium on a short-term disability policy unless you know for certain that you will go on maternity leave. It is much more difficult to build enough cash reserve for a disability that lasts multiple years and that is precisely why long-term disability insurance is a necessity.

Premiums on individual long-term disability policies are higher for women than men, especially women in their childbearing years (twenties and thirties) since the likelihood of disability is greater. Life insurance is the opposite: men's life insurance premiums are costlier than women's premiums to account for a shorter male life expectancy.

Definitions of Disability

The definition of disability greatly impacts your ability to collect full disability benefits. Any- and own-occupation definitions are the two primary types.

On one extreme, any-occupation policies are most stringent and prevent you from receiving disability benefits if you are able to work in *any* job during the disability period (even if you choose not to work). Own-occupation is the most lenient type; you receive full disability benefits even if you are working in another job throughout the disability.

Transitional own-occupation is a modified version of the own-occupation definition because you may be penalized for the salary you earn. For instance, your disability benefits will be reduced to $2,000 monthly under a transitional own-occupation policy if your disability coverage is $7,000 monthly and you're earning $5,000 monthly during the disability. Modified own-occupation coverage is similar to the any-occupation definition because you cannot receive disability benefits if you take another position during your disability.

Three Main Groups

Next, let us delve deeper into disability insurance policies for three distinct groups of people: those covered by an employer group plan, self-employed individuals or those not covered, and stay-at-home parents.

1. Covered by an employer group plan:

Consider yourself blessed if you fall into this category. Large employers usually offer short- and long-term disability policies at no cost to the employees, and 50-60 percent of pay is standard for an employer-provided long-term disability policy. If you are not paying a premium on the disability policy, you will be taxed on the income you receive when collecting disability benefits.

I have noticed that disability benefits of government employees are different from employees of large companies. Short-term disability is typically not offered since sick pay should first be exhausted, and long-term disability benefits depend on the duration of the disability. The first year of disability is covered at 60 percent, but subsequent years offer only 40 percent of pay. For this reason, government employees are encouraged to pursue supplemental policies.

If you do not feel comfortable with the level of coverage provided by your employer, you can explore supplemental long-term disability policies on your own. The insurance carrier asks about your current coverage to ensure you do not make more after-tax money as a disabled person than if you are employed.

Work with an insurance broker who specializes in disability insurance and focuses on long-term coverage. Policies and carriers differ significantly, so gain a solid understanding from the broker about the nuances of the policy, also known as riders. Salary raises provide a higher probability of underinsurance, and as a result, automatic benefit increases may be helpful but are costlier.

2. Self-employed or not covered by a group plan:
Self-employed persons and small business owners are most vulnerable to having inadequate levels of disability coverage or simply not having it at all. I have been self-employed since 2014 and am fortunate to have disability insurance through two professional organizations. One organization offers life and disability insurance policies to all its members through an outside insurance carrier. Within the group policy, members individually select a 13-week or 26-week waiting period. Longer waiting periods result in lower premiums.

Furthermore, association members may elect coverage for partial disabilities. Policies that pay during partial disability are more expensive because they do not require someone to stay out of the workforce completely when disabled, and these policies often meet the true own-occupation definition of disability.

What if you are part of a profession that does not offer group plans? Individual long-term disability policies are costly—sometimes as high as 3 percent of your income. Remember, you can control the duration of coverage. Consider delaying the benefit commencement date and limiting the duration to lower premium amounts. For instance, if the 13-week waiting period with lifetime benefit is too expensive, investigate a policy with a 26-week waiting period and up to five years of benefits. Exercise caution with this strategy: you'll need enough financial resources to support the first six months of disability and any disability that extends beyond five years.

3. Stay-at-home parent:
Presumably, you must have earnings to get disability coverage. Stay-at-home parents are not paid anything for their contribution to the household and typically would not qualify for disability coverage. Focus on maximizing the sole income earner's disability insurance coverage instead.

Health Insurance

Life and disability insurance provide valuable protections for parents. Yet, we have overlooked another crucial type of insurance: health.

Health insurance premiums and deductibles in the United States continue to rise at an unprecedented rate. For those of you fortunate enough to have employer-provided coverage, please celebrate! Even a subpar employer-sponsored plan typically offers lower premiums and better coverage than plans on the individual exchange.

Repeal of the Individual Mandate

The Tax Cuts and Jobs Act of 2017 repealed the Individual Mandate (effective 1/1/19). You no longer pay a penalty for not carrying health insurance in the US. Nevertheless, avoiding health insurance coverage altogether is risky. You will be on the hook for all medical bills, possibly ruining your credit history if you do not have cash to pay them. Medical organizations often offer payment plans but they are just like any form of debt. You should carefully analyze interest rates and the impact those payments will have on your budget.

With the Individual Mandate repeal, premiums will be even higher. People who think they are healthy enough to go without insurance may opt out, and those who are willing to pay higher premiums stay on plans due to preexisting medical conditions.

The gig economy and entrepreneurship are prevalent as technology accelerates and people increasingly opt for work-life balance. It is now uncommon to spend more than 30 years of your life working for the same company in a desk job. Faced with competing pressures of skyrocketing health insurance costs and your desire to have flexibility in your professional life, how do you move forward?

An Alternative to Traditional Insurance

Healthcare sharing programs offer an alternative to individual health insurance plans on the exchange and are often more cost effective. They are faith-based programs that facilitate voluntary sharing of eligible medical expenses among members. Examples of noneligible expenses include abortion, substance abuse, or other "unbiblical" lifestyles as determined by program guidelines. Please keep in mind that healthcare sharing programs are NOT insurance. The ministry program is not legally required to pay for a member's medical expenses. However, larger ones typically have a strong historical track record of paying eligible medical expenses once the family has met their equivalent to an annual deductible.

In full disclosure, my family moved to a healthcare sharing program in 2018 for several months, but this is not an endorsement. I heard about these programs through an XY Planning Network member forum and personally conducted extensive research on one program in particular, Medi-Share. You should diligently investigate and make your own assessment prior to selecting any healthcare sharing plan.

Four Considerations of Healthcare Sharing Plans

There are four critical questions to ask yourself prior to enrollment:

1. **Does anyone in the family have preexisting medical conditions?** Our family did not, and that was reassuring when we joined Medi-Share in 2018.

    One Medi-Share member family learned the hard way how the preexisting conditions clause worked[2]. A 35-year-old woman had $50,000 in medical bills after treatment for a cancerous tumor. Three years earlier, she had mentioned the benign growth to her doctor, who didn't suggest further treatment. Only after an appeal did Medi-Share cover her $50,000 in medical bills.

2. **Do you need coverage for preventative care visits, or are you simply seeking catastrophic assistance?** Most healthcare sharing programs do NOT cover preventative care but will theoretically

assist if an unforeseen medical emergency occurs. In that instance, other healthcare sharing program members' monthly share amounts are used for your eligible medical bills after your annual deductible equivalent is met.

If you are planning a pregnancy, remember that your out-of-pocket costs will be greater due to the sheer number of prenatal visits recommended by physicians. Many healthcare sharing programs are making their standards more stringent, requiring families to be members for a longer time period if they want maternity fees covered. This prevents a family from joining a program for a few months, getting pregnant, having the baby, and quickly leaving the plan.

3. **What is the track record for the healthcare sharing program?** Medi-Share began in 1993, and members have shared and discounted more than two billion dollars in medical bills since inception. It is one of the largest health sharing programs and has a history of paying 100 percent of eligible medical expenses beyond the Annual Household Portion. A strong track record and increasing membership count may give you additional confidence during the selection process.

4. **Does the program align with your values?** Several healthcare sharing programs do not cover "unbiblical" expenses such as abortion, birth control, and treatment related to drugs and alcohol. In fact, many programs ask you to sign an oath during the application process to confirm

that all family members agree with these biblical principles.

The Downsides of Healthcare Sharing Programs

Although healthcare sharing programs provide a nice alternative to costly medical insurance, there are two significant downsides:

1. **You don't know what you don't know.** Akin to traditional health insurance plans with high deductibles, you likely have no idea what your out-of-pocket cost will be for a procedure or prescription medication. Your level of financial responsibility is uncertain until the service is rendered, Explanation of Benefits is provided, or you picked up the prescription at the pharmacy counter. This may work in your favor, however. One of my clients on a healthcare sharing program received a substantial discount at the pharmacy counter because they did not have insurance.

   As previously mentioned, most of the healthcare sharing programs will not cover preexisting conditions. This is another negative any family should consider before joining a program.

2. **Employer-sponsored plans typically offer better value, especially at large employers.** Faith-based sharing programs are usually costlier than insurance offered by your employer but may be less expensive than plans you find on the individual exchange. My family switched to a traditional health insurance

plan as soon as my husband became eligible for benefits at his new employer in late 2018.

Personal History

Now, for a little history on my family's health insurance decisions. In 2017, my husband was employed by a large corporation with solid medical plans. Since I am self-employed, it made sense for our entire family to sign up for his employer's health insurance coverage. The premiums for our family of five ran $450 monthly for both medical and dental care. We had a well-regarded policy with a low deductible and few out-of-pocket costs.

When my husband quit his job so we could live abroad in Spain in early 2018, we sought alternate coverage. COBRA premiums would have exceeded $2,000 monthly for our family of five. On the individual exchange, medical insurance premiums still averaged $1,500 monthly for silver or bronze level policies with much higher deductibles. The government's premium assistance only happens at certain income levels, and we did not have a clear idea of what our family's income would be that year. We would have tripled our medical insurance cost by pursuing one of the individual exchange plans.

Healthcare sharing programs were a saving grace for our family. Our monthly premium (known as the "monthly share amount" by Medi-Share) was $788, and our annual household deductible ("annual household portion") was $3,000. Our regular doctors were within the program's preferred provider network. The healthcare sharing program negotiated a discount directly with the medical provider and sent me an Explanation of Sharing after the service was rendered. Then the medical provider billed me directly.

When my husband became employed again in August 2018, our entire family switched from Medi-Share to his employer's health insurance plan. The new plan is more cost effective and covers incidentals such as flu shots. Even though we are now on a high deductible health insurance plan, we still pay less out-of-pocket for doctor office or urgent care visits than we did under Medi-Share.

Do Your Homework

Healthcare sharing programs are not intended for everyone. **Traditional health insurance is often the best option for many families, particularly for individuals with preexisting medical conditions.** But if you are frustrated with traditional insurance and had no familiarity with these programs prior to reading this book, I encourage you to conduct additional research. The four largest healthcare sharing programs in 2018 were:
- Christian Healthcare Ministries (CHM)
- Liberty HealthShare
- Medi-Share
- Samaritan Ministries

If you are still torn between a healthcare sharing program and traditional insurance, consider visiting the website of Take Command Health[3]. They act as an online health insurance broker for families, helping you compare traditional policies with sharing programs like Medi-Share.

You Cannot Emergency Proof Your Life

Risk extends beyond an investment portfolio. You cannot emergency proof your life, but insurers take on risk in exchange for a monetary premium you pay them. Comprehensive financial planners often evaluate your insurance levels in conjunction with the broader financial plan.

As evidenced by this chapter, there are nuances to insurance, and we did not touch on them all. Long-term care, along with property and casualty, are two other common types of insurance that fall outside the scope of this book.

As a fee-only fiduciary advisor, my only source of compensation comes directly from clients through a transparent fee. There is absolutely no financial incentive for me to recommend healthcare sharing programs, Take Command Health, a particular insurance provider, or level of insurance coverage. I am mentioning these resources because they may help you live a richer life. And remember, even the faithful have insurance!

Chapter Nine

Traditional Retirement Isn't the Answer

Many people think retirement and financial independence are synonymous. They're wrong.

Traditional "retirement" means you work until age 65 and leave the workforce entirely. Financial independence reframes this historical perspective of retirement and refers to a time when you no longer *have* to work for money. Increasingly, there are people who worked hard in their twenties and thirties but lived frugally enough to become financially independent at a young age. They are part of the FIRE movement, which stands for Financial Independence, Retire Early.

Many of them are now online bloggers in true "Sherpa" fashion: They reached the top of the mountain and are teaching others to do the same. They leverage time to share important information with their audience but still slow down and enjoy a simpler life.

Peter Adeney, more commonly known as Mr. Money Mustache, is a Canadian born blogger. He and his wife studied engineering and computer science and worked in tech-industry cubicle jobs in the late 1990s and early 2000s. They saved aggressively in passive index funds and real estate investments, achieving an early retirement in 2005 to start a family. Six years into retirement, Mr. Money Mustache became increasingly frustrated with friends and former coworkers living ridiculously expensive lifestyles while sacrificing long-term financial freedom. He started a blog in 2011 to share his secrets of financial independence, and it is one of the most popular FIRE blogs today.

The FIRE movement is growing rapidly, and for good reason. Several millennials and Gen Xers are frustrated with the old school mentality of work. They want to find meaning through work and are willing to pursue unconventional career paths. For them, it isn't about fully retiring at age 35 or 40. Rather, it is achieving financial independence early and opening the door for volunteerism or career fields that don't pay well.

Regardless of whether retirement or financial independence is your end goal, you will need a solid financial foundation to make it happen.

There Is No Magic Number

To be financially independent, my number is going to differ from yours. If your mortgage is paid off, you have no debt, your kids are grown, and you live frugally, you'll need less money than me to reach financial independence. My kids are young. My family still has a mortgage. Our living expenses will continue to be high for the next 20 years. We need to amass more than you for financial independence.

As a financial advisor, I cannot tell you that one million dollars or two million dollars is "enough." Each situation is unique, and there are too many variables. The average US life expectancy is 78.7 years, according to World Bank. My financial planning software uses 95 as the average life expectancy for a woman and 90 for the average life expectancy of a man because people may live well beyond the average. What if you live to 100? Or 110?

With technology advances, medical research and development is exploding. Cancer patients and people with heart disease have a wider variety of available drugs and procedures. Transplants have come a long way. Preventative vaccines make diseases like polio or tetanus practically nonexistent.[1]

Despite medical advances, however, the average US life expectancy actually nudged lower[2]. The number of deaths from substance abuse and suicide has increased. About 115 people in the US die each day from opioid overdose, and six people die each day from alcohol abuse. This statistic is both alarming and sad. What can we do about it?

Let's ponder this Bible verse:

> "For I know the plans I have for you, declares the Lord, plans for welfare and not for evil, to give you a future and a hope."
> –Jeremiah 29:11

Depression and anxiety are serious issues that pervade our society. Anxiety is the most common mental illness, and 6.7 percent of American adults admitted having at least one depressive episode in the last year[3]. Retirees who were previously driven by work may feel like they have nothing left when the workday is removed.

That's why purposeful living is so important. Try to be intentional with time, talent, and treasure so you can bring your best self to others. Christians should wrap their identities in Jesus, not in the tasks they accomplish at work.

In his book, *The New Retirementality*[4], Mitch Anthony reiterates that retirement isn't about a number. Rather, it's a shift in attitude. Plenty of people retire at 65 without adequate savings and are forced back into work because social security is not enough. Others, who are financially secure, continue working past age 65 simply because they enjoy what they are doing. I'd argue that the latter group has it much better.

I've Got Rhythm, I've Got Music

When fully retired, there is a new rhythm to your days. You do not have to get dressed up or rush to an 8 a.m. meeting. Time is no longer a scarce resource. In fact, how you fill the time will have a far greater impact on your level of happiness.

Although I never "retired," I was a stay-at-home mom for a few months. My idealistic dream of this time with a four-year-old and a baby was crushed within the first few weeks. Working outside the home, I felt a sense of purpose. I'd go to work with a smile on my face and could accomplish things. Real things, for others. I could craft an investment strategy, implement an estate plan, help a college grad budget, or review a tax return. All of these activities made me feel capable and valued.

As a stay-at-home mother, I felt that my parenting skills were never good enough. My husband would come home from a long day at work and find a messy house. There were no important emails or phone calls requiring my immediate attention, and the silence became deafening. I rarely left the

Traditional Retirement Isn't the Answer

house for fear that one of the boys would miss a nap. On the few occasions we ventured out, it was difficult to engage in meaningful conversation with other stay-at-home parents.

I'm not the Pinterest-perfect mom. On the rare occasions I bake, it's brownie mix or premade cookie dough. My idea of decorating for a party involves buying themed plates and streamers.

But I do know that God put me on earth to help others, and my work as a CPA financial planner is an extension of that purpose. I also know that I'm worthy of God's love, perfectly and wonderfully created by Him. No qualifiers. No judgment.

When you wrap your identity in worldly things, there will always be a gaping hole in your heart. Instead, clothe yourself in God's grace. Give yourself compassion for any wrongdoing and remember that holiness is possible.

"Whatever you do, work at it with all your heart." That's the colorful saying next to my desk. Your mission in life doesn't stop at age 65 or two million dollars. If your day job brings excitement and helps you get out of bed in the morning, keep doing it. Do it until you're blue in the face. That doesn't mean you have to work full time or cannot travel. Once you have reached financial independence, part-time or seasonal work may be a better expression of your talents.

If traditional work isn't the answer, consider becoming a volunteer. You dictate your level of involvement and choose to work with the charitable organizations that are most meaningful to you. If you are widowed, perhaps you can lead a widow support group. Join Habitat for Humanity if you enjoy working with your hands and constructing things. If you want to help homeless expectant mothers, volunteer at a maternity center. The possibilities are endless!

You may say you are too old or too young to live in alignment with your life's purpose.

Here's the truth: age does not matter one bit.

Winston Churchill was 65 when he went to war against Hitler as Britain's prime minister.

Michelangelo was 72 when he designed the dome of St. Peter's Basilica in Rome.

Nelson Mandela was elected president of South Africa and awarded the Nobel Peace Prize at age 75.

Sister Madonna Buder, a Roman Catholic nun, completed the Ironman at age 76.

John Glenn traveled into space at age 77.

At age 91, Frank Lloyd Wright finished his work on the Guggenheim Museum.

> You may say you are too old or too young to live in alignment with your life's purpose. Here's the truth: age does not matter one bit.

Financial Independence Examples

Hopefully, you agree that traditional retirement isn't the answer. Financial independence allows you to use God-given gifts to serve others. Below are a few examples of clients who pursued financial independence early.

Dave & Cindy

Dave is a successful partner at a large public accounting firm. He and his wife, Cindy, have four children, ranging in age from three to twelve. Dave's job is stressful, and it feels as though he never has enough time at home with his family. Cindy stays at home with the kids but is college educated and willing to return to the paid workforce if Dave retires early or moves into a less stressful position. Dave recently turned 40, and his company offers a generous pension benefit if he stays until age 46.

To Dave, retirement isn't about leaving the workplace permanently. He wants to find a less stressful position that values his expertise. If he can't find this, Dave wants to volunteer at his kids' schools and find other ways to fulfill God's plan for his life.

Dave and Cindy have a detailed budget and have already amassed $1.65 million. They expect to add over $140,000 annually to investment accounts if Dave continues to work in his current role. We are running different scenarios to see if Dave could leave the accounting firm sooner than 46. This includes adjusting living expenses and increasing Cindy's income.

Jon & Katie

Jon is a long-time government employee, and his wife, Katie, has worked in hospital administration for several years. Jon has the option of retiring as early as age 50; mandatory retirement occurs at age 57. His pension benefit is more lucrative the longer he stays.

Jon and Katie have jointly amassed more than one million dollars of investable assets and follow a detailed budget. Katie is exploring other career options. Although they seek financial independence early, neither Jon nor Katie want to stop working entirely. We spend time in meetings discussing both Jon and Katie's second careers.

Mike & Michelle

Mike enjoyed a military career and transitioned to a financially lucrative role in the private sector a few years ago. At age 55, Mike is interested in becoming a commercial pilot, and the starting pay is much lower than his current role. Most pilots need to spend at least one or two years working for a lesser-known regional airline before they can move to legacy brands like Southwest or Delta. He plans to retire as a pilot at age 65.

Technically, Mike could fully retire today. He and Michelle have amassed enough in savings to likely cover their living expenses until age 100. Mike's military pension and future social security income help as well. However, Mike doesn't WANT to retire now. He is a man of faith and feels called to be a commercial pilot. He wants to transport passengers from one destination to the next. That is financial independence.

As you can see, each of these clients have individual perspectives and goals surrounding financial independence. Yet in each instance, they have to follow a similar path to reach it. Let's turn our attention away from them for a moment and focus on you. What are your goals? Why do you want to "retire?" Can you reframe retirement as financial independence? If not, what is holding you back?

Redefine Retirement

I'm okay opposing commonly-held societal beliefs. This chapter is no exception. Rather than just tell you why society's view of retirement is wrong, I'm going to show you how to redefine retirement.

1. Uncover your why:

You were made for more. There is a special purpose for your life. What is the unique contribution you can make to the world?

There isn't a perfect answer. We are at different points in the journey of uncovering our mission. But the sooner you gain clarity around this higher purpose, the sooner you can pursue goals. The sooner you can make an impact.

If you're having difficulty during this step, take some of author Jeff Goins' advice from *The Art of Work: A Proven Path to Discovering What You Were Meant to Do*.

First, observe and listen. If you come across someone else who has found her calling, pay attention to what is present in her life, and what might be missing from yours. Notice the subtle things that make you come alive. A calling typically isn't a momentary epiphany but rather a series of experiences that tap into your strengths. Learn from mentors. Get your mindset right by focusing on abundant, not scarce, opportunities. Then, practice your skills often. How do athletes make it to the professional level? Mindset, skill, and practice. That's how.

When you're ready to act on your calling, build a bridge instead of taking one gigantic leap. Any intentional change I've made has been carefully contemplated. Before leaving my job in 2013 and becoming a stay-at-home mom, I talked with my husband, Bryan, and confirmed we could pay our bills on a single income. It wasn't until a few years later that I started WorthyNest® and began living my professional calling.

Pursuing God's will for your life inevitably entails failure. Treating those failures as learning opportunities, or pivot points, enables you to push forward and act out your dream. Building WorthyNest® from scratch hasn't been all rainbows and butterflies. There have been several successes and setbacks. But it does not mean I'll be closing shop anytime soon.

Your calling isn't a destination. It's a journey. Dig deep to uncover your WHY.

2. Think first:

Brainstorm. Drawing on your WHY, consider the roles that could position you to pursue your life's mission. Is it a flexible or part-time role in a related industry? Is it volunteering your time to help others in need? Explore the possibilities, and don't be afraid to think outside the box.

Social entrepreneurship is growing in popularity. People (just like you and me) recognize a social, cultural, or environmental problem and launch businesses to solve those problems.

While large for-profit companies are primarily focused on revenue and shareholder return, not-for-profits use revenue to advance social causes. Social entrepreneurs typically follow a hybrid model. They are deeply passionate about eradicating poverty, providing healthcare worldwide, or taking on some other cause with social impact. The social entrepreneur will reinvest profits into an important cause. With the Internet, entrepreneurship is no longer reserved for gregarious salesmen. You can emotionally connect with other people thousands of miles away who share similar values.

For instance, Certified B Corps are taking social entrepreneurship to a whole new level. B Corps are for-profit companies certified by the nonprofit B Lab to meet social and environmental standards around performance, accountability, and transparency[5]. These hybrid companies are popping up in more than 50 countries and 130 industries.

Becoming an entrepreneur isn't the only way to make an impact. Consider other alternatives, using your innate skills. If you play an instrument and your kids are grown, maybe you can teach music in the evenings and on the weekends. This is part-time work you can start even before you are financially independent.

The critical component isn't to uncover a financially lucrative calling. Instead, pinpoint the profession or activity that makes you come alive. Think about the impact your profession could have on the community and world.

3. **Put pen to paper:**
Once you have clearly identified your higher calling, it's time to put pen to paper and see if this is financially viable. Do market research. This step will obviously be easier if you will be moving from full-time to part-time work in the same role. If you're earning $100,000 and want to work 60 percent in the future, expect your salary to be $60,000. Also, factor in the benefits you lose by moving to a part-time arrangement.

Many companies require an 80 percent workload for benefit eligibility, including health insurance and retirement match. If you are under age 65 and not eligible for Medicare, expect insurance premiums to skyrocket unless you are able to switch to a spouse's employer plan or move to one of the healthcare sharing plans discussed in Chapter 8.

Thoroughly research salary expectations if you decide to transition to a new career field like my client Mike. New pilots working for regional airlines earn $54,000 on average[6], while experienced pilots working for major commercial airlines can expect earnings of $130,000 and above. Multi-year cash projections in Excel can be especially helpful as you map out future income and expenses.

Suppose you decide to become an entrepreneur during this financial independence stage. Most businesses generate a loss in the first year and do not break even until year two or beyond. At a minimum, expect to live on your investment portfolio or spouse's earnings during the first three years. It may take five years or more before your take-home pay matches your former salary.

4. **Give yourself permission:**
Simply because you decide on one plan doesn't mean you must follow it. If you are five years away from being financially independent, your interests and passions may change. Give yourself permission to change the plan.

Suppose your targeted financial independence date is eight years away but you are in a job you hate. Rather than stick out a grueling eight years, find out if you can go into a career more fulfilling but with a pay cut. This may mean extending the financial independence goal to 10 or 12 years. That is perfectly fine. You may not want to leave the other career 12 years from now!

Retirement at 65 Isn't the Answer

Age doesn't define you or the contribution you can make to society. Fully retiring at age 65 may stifle you and the gifts you can share with others. Think carefully about your second act using the Redefine Retirement framework if you are able to become financially independent at an early age.

Also, don't be afraid to change careers. My husband did it at age 36 and couldn't be happier with his decision. What are you waiting for?

Chapter Ten

Go for Broke

Many Christians say that money is the root of all evil and use a bible quote to defend their position. I don't believe money itself is the root of all evil. The *love* of money—at the expense of a relationship with the Lord—is sinful.

The more money I earn, the more I'm able to give back. Greed is certainly a sin, and excessive greed quickly becomes evil. But it's quite possible (even as Christians) to enhance monetary wealth without letting greed dictate our hearts' desires.

Tithing

Are you familiar with the concept of tithing? It is introduced as law in Leviticus 27:30-34,

> "Every tithe of the land, whether of the seed of the land or of the fruit of the trees, is the Lord's; it is holy to the Lord. If a man wishes to redeem some of his tithe, he shall add a fifth to it.

And every tithe of herds and flocks, every tenth animal of all that pass under the herdsman's staff, shall be holy to the Lord. One shall not differentiate between good or bad, neither shall he make a substitute for it; and if he does substitute for it, then both it and the substitute shall be holy; it shall not be redeemed."

Tithe literally means tenth. The first 10 percent is considered holy, belonging to God. Christians are called to give 10 percent of their income back to the church. Catholics are also Christians but take a slightly liberal stance on who should benefit from that 10 percent. For instance, Catholics might only give 5 percent to the church but another 5 percent to charitable organizations that feed the hungry, provide shelter for the homeless, or treat medical ailments.

Don't feel compelled to stop at 10 percent. If you're in a position to give more than 10 percent, do it! One of my clients gives 25 percent of his physician's salary to church and other charitable causes. He is passionate about the work he does as a doctor and feels abundantly blessed to give more.

Now for a confession: Tithing wasn't even on my radar in my twenties or early thirties. I'm a cradle Catholic, having grown up in the Catholic church since birth. My parents put checks in the collection basket weekly at church, but we never really discussed the dollar amount relative to their earnings. As a young adult, I prioritized giving but did not expend energy on determining the right donation amount. Since we now understand tithing, Bryan and I consistently give the first 10 percent to God.

> "No one can serve two masters. Either you will hate the one and love the other, or you will be devoted to the one and despise the other. You cannot serve both God and money."
>
> – Matthew 6:24

It is never too late to start tithing, as evidenced by my personal example. If you're currently giving 2 percent and want to get to 10 percent, realign your budget with your intentions. Take a hard look at areas you can cut (e.g. entertainment or dining out) and increase charitable contributions accordingly. You may not get to the 10 percent level immediately but stick with it and track your progress. Allocate a portion of bonuses or tax refunds to charitable giving, too.

Maximize Charitable Contributions

We briefly touched on charitable giving in a prior chapter, but I only spoke about it in the context of a line item on a detailed personal budget. Below are five ways that US taxpayers can maximize charitable contributions:

1. **Make non-cash gifts part of your giving plan.**

You have probably donated household items and clothing to charities in the past. Are you keeping a detailed list of the items being donated, their thrift shop fair market value, the original purchase price, and the donation date? If not, you're overlooking important tax documentation according to IRS Publication 526[1]. It needn't take a long time to compile the list. For example, Goodwill issues tax receipts when you drop off donations in person. Feel free to use estimates such as $50 for a bag of 10 T-shirts.

Looking for another non-cash option? Gift appreciated stock that is sitting in a taxable brokerage account. This means you won't pay long-term capital gains tax on the stock appreciation. Please note that the strategy doesn't work for retirement accounts.

Let's suppose you want to make a $1,000 donation, and you've held $1,000 of General Electric stock for more than a year. Your cost basis in the stock is only $600. Rather than selling the stock and incurring $400 of long-term capital gains, you give the stock directly to the charity. The charitable organization is not required to pay capital gains tax due to its nonprofit status. You still receive a $1,000 charitable deduction and avoid paying $80 in capital gains tax ($400 gain multiplied by an assumed 20 percent federal and state tax rate).

2. **Create impact with your contributions.**

You likely have a big heart and want to give to several different causes. Yet, there are so *many* valuable causes in the world. Your contribution will go further if you select a *few* causes and give meaningfully to them. Consider using the search tool within Charity Navigator[2] for independent rankings on the nonprofit's level of transparency and accountability.

Your time is more valuable than writing 50 different $100 checks and tracking them for income tax purposes. Furthermore, you can get more involved with the charity's mission and perhaps serve on the board. You will know where your dollars are going, and you understand the direct impact your donation has on each intended recipient.

Another viable option—for small business owners only—is to partner with an organization like Good Meets World[3], a community founded by Zach Tucker. It consists of like-minded business owners who are connected to a charitable cause and each other. The businesses are networking, giving, volunteering, and changing the world together. My wealth management firm WorthyNest® donates a portion of profits to support St. Louis Crisis Nursery. Since my firm's focus is families, I felt called to support local families in need. St. Louis Crisis Nursery offers short-term housing and childcare annually to about 6,500 children whose families face an emergency caused by illness, homelessness, or domestic violence.

3. Open a donor-advised fund.

If creating impact resonates with you, a donor-advised fund[4] ("DAF") may be a wonderful method to carry out your charitable intentions. I've helped many families put philanthropic strategies in place, and the donor-advised fund is my vehicle of choice because it's simple and easy.

Donor-advised funds are ideal if you have not already committed a specific dollar amount to a charity in writing and you want to give substantially to multiple charities.

Alternatively, DAFs are powerful when you sell a business and want to establish a philanthropic legacy.

Fidelity allows you to open a DAF for as little as $5,000. You make an initial contribution (i.e. cash, stock, or mutual fund) and select one or more of the DAF's pre-approved investment options. The charitable contribution is immediately deductible, even if you delay a charitable grant request until a subsequent tax year. When you are ready to distribute money to charity, contact the DAF sponsor (e.g. Fidelity) and submit a grant request. You can make multiple grant requests if you wish to support several charities.

4. Carefully contemplate timing.

Many people make donations in the last few weeks of the year, but nonprofits have needs throughout the year. Some nonprofits even promote Giving Tuesday[5], a global giving movement held the Tuesday after Thanksgiving to spur giving outside of December.

Think about donating at an untraditional time like spring or summer. If you insist on cash gifts, enroll in automatic monthly or quarterly payments to the charitable institution. This smooths cash flow for both you and the charity.

5. Stack deductions in one tax year:

The Tax Cuts and Jobs Act of 2017 has substantial implications for US families, and nonprofits are concerned that charitable giving will go down with the enhanced standard deduction. With proper planning, you can fulfill your philanthropic goals and still get an income tax benefit.

If you are close to the new $24,000 standard deduction threshold as a married couple (or $12,000 standard deduction as a single person), consider doubling or tripling your charitable contributions in a particular tax year. You'll itemize deductions in the year you maximize charitable contributions and then resort to the standard deduction in the subsequent tax year. Donor-advised funds, illustrated above, are especially beneficial if you want to "stack" charitable donations. You take the tax deduction in the year you contribute to the donor-advised fund, regardless of when the charity receives a grant.

Make It a Family Affair

Furthermore, donor-advised funds are an excellent way to involve the whole family in charitable giving. Young adult children can be authorized on the account and begin to have a say in where the money goes. If you have more than one child on the account, you could either divvy up the total anticipated grant among the children *OR* let each child have responsibility for a particular grant year (e.g. 2020, 2021, and 2022). One of my friends in her early sixties used this technique with her adult kids and found the conversations so enlightening. One child wanted to give to animal shelters, while the other felt passionate about eradicating homelessness.

If you have younger children, a donor-advised fund may still be an effective tool. You don't need to name the child as an authorized individual to engage in similar types of conversations about charitable giving.

Be patient with your little ones. Understand not all kids have a natural inclination to give back to others. As parents, it's our duty to identify our core values and pass those same values down to children. Any dollar amount, no matter how small, can instill generosity in kids. It's when we practice that pattern over and over that it finally becomes habit.

Charity Begins at Home

I grew up Catholic and attended Catholic grade school, high school, and even college. One of the things I vividly remember from grade school is the motto, "Respect, Spirituality, and Responsibility."

We were instructed to give of our time, talent, and treasure to uphold the principle of spirituality. Treasure, or financial generosity, is only one element of giving. Time and talent are just as significant.

When you give your time to those in need, you are showing genuine compassion and concern for others. You may want to serve on an advisory board or junior board of a nonprofit organization. Fundraising is often part of that role, and you may even be able to use natural talents to raise money for an excellent cause. If board involvement isn't your cup of tea, you may prefer to volunteer by serving meals to homeless people, watching children at a nursery, organizing clothes at Goodwill, or packing nonperishables for a food pantry.

Volunteering provides a tremendous opportunity for your children to get involved, too. Find out if your preferred charitable organization offers family-friendly volunteer events. There are countless ways to share your talents, or those of your children, with others.

Are you great at sewing? Consider knitting hats for cancer patients.

Are you wonderful with animals? Offer to help at your local animal shelter.

Do you have a beautiful singing voice? Sing in the church choir or worship group.

Is sports your forte? Coach your daughter's soccer team.

Are you a great conversationalist? Play checkers at a senior living community.

Does organizing come naturally to you? Spearhead a coat drive in early winter.

The opportunities are endless. Make service a priority in your family and stick to it.

Especially around the holidays, there are ample opportunities at church, school, and within your local community to be generous. Grab an extra box of stuffing or can of soup at the grocery store for a food drive. Buy an extra pair of gloves or mittens for a children's shelter. Adopt a family at Christmas so the adults and kids in that family will have something under the tree this year.

Now is the time to think radically about causes that are near and dear to your heart.

The Ice Bucket Challenge became an overnight phenomenon in 2014, when Pat Quinn brought a charitable splash-fest to his Quinn for the Win Facebook page. The image of dumping a bucket of ice and water on another person's head brought instant awareness to amyotrophic lateral sclerosis (ALS), also known as Lou Gehrig's disease. Supporters raised more than $115 million for The ALS Association[6] in just two months, accelerating momentum toward the search for treatments and a cure.

Chris Marlow's book, *Doing Good Is Simple,* recounts the early days of his nonprofit organization Help One Now and provides tangible ways to start serving. Marlow says there are three main hurdles to doing good:

1. The issues are too numerous.
2. The problems are too big.
3. The solutions are too complicated.

Each hurdle represents an excuse. To jump over these hurdles, Marlow offers six suggestions:

1. Do something rather than nothing.
2. Start small.
3. Follow your passions.
4. Use your gifts.
5. Build relationships.
6. Stick with it.

These principles are universal.

Should We Really Give It All Away?

Luke 12: 32-34 states,

> *"Fear not, little flock, for it is your Father's good pleasure to give you the kingdom.* **Sell your possessions and give to the needy.** *Provide yourselves with moneybags that do not grow old, where no thief approaches and no moth destroys. For where your treasure is, there will your heart also be."*

Micah Bales of Red Letter Christians[7] analyzed these words and carefully concluded that we cannot serve both God and money. The author acknowledges that his deepest fear isn't losing material possessions but rather lack of autonomy.

Can you relate? Are you afraid of asking others for help if catastrophe strikes? Do you prioritize self-sufficiency over community?

Go for Broke

We don't *need* to sell all of our possessions to enter heaven. However, there is a dichotomy between comfort and transformation. Christians are called to transformation. God wants to completely transform our lives. Not bits and pieces. Not smoothing the rough edges. REAL transformation.

How can we be transformed if we live within our comfort zone?

Stagnancy or maintaining the status quo may *feel* comfortable but it means we aren't living up to our full potential.

Living richly means taking all that is given to us and using it for good…

Improving the lives of those around us…

Helping the sick and those in despair…

Acting as strong role models…

Embodying love in every interaction…

"Go for broke" means pouring your heart out to others in a life-giving way.

It means uncovering your true purpose and aligning your actions with higher-level aspirations.

It's leaving the world better off than when you came into it. Will you go for broke?

Chapter Eleven

Get Your Affairs in Order

(You'll Thank Me Later)

What is inevitable but a topic that no one wants to discuss? Death.

It's the truth, my friend.

Christians know that our eternal life resides with our Father in heaven, but many of us do not want to think about the day that our time on earth is done.

Tragedies happen every day. Every hour. Every minute. It's impossible for us to predict the future. But that doesn't mean we can ignore the fact that death is one certainty of life.

People get estate documents to put plans in place for when they die or are no longer capable of making decisions themselves. Estate planning isn't exclusively reserved for the affluent.

As parents, it's our duty to protect our children and provide a warm, loving environment for them. If something tragic happens to you, who will take care of your children?

Jeff's Experience as a Beneficiary

My friend, Jeff, is an only child. Jeff's parents divorced when he went out-of-state to college. A few years later, his dad died unexpectedly of a heart attack.

Jeff and his father were really close. When Jeff lost his father, part of his soul died as well. The next several months were extremely hard on him.

Processing grief and other strong emotions after death is difficult. But settling an estate is also challenging. Jeff's father didn't have any estate documents. All remaining assets passed to Jeff, since he was an only child and his parents were divorced.

Jeff's dad saved more than one million dollars. As a grieving 20-something, it takes a lot of strength to sit with that money and not spend it frivolously.

The investment advisory firm that managed money for Jeff's father was more than happy to continue managing the inherited investment portfolio for their standard advisory fee, totaling thousands of dollars.

As Jeff's friend, I sat down with him and reviewed the portfolio in detail. I told Jeff about expense ratios, hidden 12b1 fees, investment benchmarks, and other key financial concepts. Most of the portfolio consisted of expensive mutual funds that did not outperform their benchmarks.

A whole new world opened to Jeff. Before his dad's death, Jeff had no interest in finances. Now, he regularly checks the portfolio and researches stocks. Jeff amicably left the expensive investment advisor and began managing his own portfolio at a low-cost custodian.

Jeff also shared with me a dream he had about using some of the money to honor his father's memory through travel. I thought it was an excellent idea. Jeff and his girlfriend took a one-year hiatus from work and traveled around the world. He cultivated a love for photography deep in Africa's oldest national park and proposed to his girlfriend along the Great Wall of China.

Travel helped Jeff move into the next phase of life as a married man and eventually a father. I'm grateful I could serve as a sounding board on Jeff's financial questions after his dad's death.

But not everyone will have a confidante who can alleviate financial concerns if a parent prematurely passes away. And so, it's worth repeating the question:

If something tragic happens to you, who will take care of your children?

If you are married and something happens to both of you, how will you know that your children are well provided for?

Life insurance is only one piece of the puzzle, and we already discussed that in Chapter 8. If you are pregnant or have any children under the age of 18, I strongly encourage you to get a Last Will and Testament, at a minimum. It's a legal document that spells out who gets custody of your children if you (and your spouse, if applicable) die.

8 Reasons to Get Estate Documents Now

Why get your estate in order? Emily Kirk of Kirk Estate Planning based in St. Louis offers eight reasons why you should create a will or trust[1]:

#1 - Peace for Everyone
This is perhaps the most important aspect of estate planning. Planning ahead provides you with peace of mind and helps ensure harmony in your family. This can be more valuable than money as far as maintaining relationships.

#2 – Provide for Your Family
Without an estate plan in place, your family may get less, and it will take them longer to get it. This means your loved ones will be left in limbo and might end up without enough money to pay bills and other living expenses. It's not uncommon for families with an unexpected death to experience severe stress due to financial strain in the weeks, months, and years to come.

#3 – Keep Your Children Safe
As unpleasant as this next thought is going to be, take a minute and ask yourself what would happen to your kids if you and/or your spouse were involved in a major car accident on the way home from work tomorrow? If you don't have an estate plan in place, you might not like the answer to that question. The courts will have to sort out who will serve as your children's guardian, but why leave that decision up to the courts at all?

#4 – Minimize Your Expenses
When you die without an estate plan (and without a living trust, in particular), the courts are forced to handle everything: Distribution of your property, guardianship of your children, and dissolution of your business. This is known as probate, and it can get very expensive—thousands of dollars for even

modest estates. That's money your family could have used for living expenses and other bills.

#5 – Get Property to Loved Ones Quickly

Using the probate process, your family might have to wait anywhere from three to nine months to get anything after you die. With a good estate plan such as a living trust, your family will have access to money they need to pay monthly expenses, funeral costs, outstanding medical bills, and anything else they need right away and without delay.

#6 – Save Your Family from the Difficult Decisions

Can you imagine trying to decide when to pull the plug on a parent who is in a coma or similar condition? Or deciding how his or her remains should be handled? Those are heartbreaking decisions that no one should have to face. You can specify in your estate plan how you want end-of-life care to be handled and what kind of arrangements you want made for your remains.

#7 – Plan for Incapacity

Estate planning is not just about death. It's very common for people to become incapacitated by an accident or sudden medical episode—like a stroke—that leaves them unable to manage their financial affairs. If this happens to you, who will take care of paying your bills or managing your healthcare? A power of attorney designation for both financial and healthcare decisions can save your family a lot of time and money.

#8 – Support Your Favorite Cause

You might have heard that Mark Zuckerberg (the founder of Facebook) decided to join Bill Gates and Warren Buffet in leaving the vast majority of his fortune to charity instead of his family. Even if you don't have billions of dollars to leave to charity, you can still make a difference by supporting your favorite educational, religious, or other charitable cause. Without an estate plan, none of your money will go to charity.

Estate Planning Lingo

Since I live in Missouri, most of the examples used here will be based on Missouri law. Each state has different laws regarding probate avoidance, spousal property rights, and estate and inheritance taxes.

If you die tomorrow without a will, a guardian will be appointed for your minor children and all assets without a specific beneficiary designation go through a very public process called probate.

If you have a will, the probate process is still relevant. Your **Last Will and Testament** explains to the probate court exactly who will care for your children, who is in charge of implementing your wishes (also called the executor), and how your property will be distributed.

Beneficiary designations indicate how certain assets will be distributed, even if there is no Last Will and Testament. For example, if I list my husband as 100 percent primary beneficiary on my life insurance policy, the life insurance proceeds will pass directly to him at my death. If Bryan isn't alive when I pass away, the contingent beneficiary designation is important. My kids could be listed as contingent beneficiaries, but that's not ideal. My children shouldn't have one million dollars or more in life insurance proceeds at their disposal. Creating a **revocable trust** and listing the trust as 100 percent contingent beneficiary solves the problem.

Some families opt for revocable, or living, trusts that offer greater asset protection and privacy. However, trusts are more expensive to create than basic wills. You still have some control over how debts are paid and assets are divided through a will, but trusts have a greater likelihood of helping families preserve financial wealth for multiple generations. Most estate attorneys recommend revocable trusts for parents with minor children.

Revocable means you can change or revoke the terms of the trust while you are still alive. If you have a joint revocable trust and your spouse passes away, refer to the trust details to see if you can still make changes to the trust.

Irrevocable trusts are set in stone. It is very difficult to change them unless you have a trust protector. Families with significant taxable estates often use irrevocable trusts as a holding place for permanent life insurance policies so there are no income or estate tax implications when the insured dies. Establishing an irrevocable trust involves additional cost both at the beginning and during the term of trust.

When you hire an estate attorney to prepare a will and/or trust, any reputable estate attorney will advise you to have a **Healthcare Directive** (also called Living Will), **Medical Power of Attorney (POA)** and **HIPAA Release**, and **Financial Power of Attorney**. The Medical POA and Healthcare Directives are essential when you can no longer make medical decisions for yourself. Your spouse is typically listed as the Power of Attorney if you're married. Most opt for an adult child, family friend, or other relative to serve as a backup Power of Attorney.

Financial Powers of Attorney ensure your bills are paid and other financial matters are addressed if you are incapacitated. Powers of Attorney are critical when you are still alive but unable to make medical or financial decisions due to physical and/or cognitive decline. If you pass away, the Power of Attorney is no longer relevant.

The Last Will and Testament (and trust, if you created one) will define who handles your estate and financial matters. In the case of a will, the person is known as **Executor**. A **Trustee** will handle financial matters following your death according to the terms of the trust. When selecting an executor (and Trustee, if applicable), consider the person's level of conscientiousness.

Guardians and Trustees

Ensuring adequate care for minor children if you pass away prematurely is critical. Your Last Will and Testament will appoint a guardian who cares for the children in your absence. If you're married, this duty will naturally fall to your spouse.

But for those who aren't married or want to consider backup guardians, family members and close friends are usually good choices.

Think about the history you have with a particular family member. If you have a solid relationship with your mother or father, you may want to choose them as guardian. But you must be cognizant of the lifestyle your parent leads. Is your parent physically and emotionally able to take care of your children in their sixties, seventies or eighties? Will acting as a guardian change their pace of life in a positive or negative way?

Perhaps an adult sibling would be a better fit. Bryan and I signed our estate documents right before we had our oldest son. We ultimately choose Bryan's older sister as guardian. She already had one son, and we knew she and her husband could provide a safe, loving environment for our son. My only sister wasn't married and had no children when we signed the estate documents. Additionally, she lives four hours away from us in Kansas City. We didn't select our parents as guardians for two reasons:

1. It would be hard to choose between the two sets of grandparents without hurting the other grandparents' feelings.
2. We knew both sets of grandparents would want to retire within 10 years of our son's birth and thought taking care of a grandchild may be more of a burden during retirement.

In hindsight, we choose wisely. My parents are both retired and have had major medical issues within the last few years. It's physically hard for them to spend more than a few days with our three rambunctious boys. Bryan's mom and dad love to travel, and having young kids in tow may limit their ability to travel to exotic destinations.

Ultimately, the decision to choose a guardian for your child(ren) is yours. Hopefully, I offered some perspective on guardian selection that an attorney may not review with you.

If you move forward with a Revocable Trust, the Trustee must follow the terms of the trust to ensure any life insurance proceeds or other financial assets are used and distributed equitably.

This may come as a surprise: the Trustee and guardian do not need to be the same person.

Your minor children will live with the guardian and follow the guardian's house rules. If you insist on sending kids to private elementary or high school, money will come out of the trust—and the Trustee is accountable for financial matters once you are deceased. The home environment should be independent of the finances.

Some of my clients have a trustworthy sister who would be a great guardian but isn't responsible with money. The couple worked hard to scrimp and save, and they don't want the sister's Achilles heel to impact the kids if they pass away. In this case, they may consider listing the sister as guardian and selecting a different Trustee.

Remember, estate planning documents are focused on long-term, rather than short-term, needs. Selecting an initial guardian and trustee (especially if you are an unmarried parent) can be challenging. But it's also important.

Eventually, your minor children will be adults. If you've gone through the trouble of creating a trust, think about an appropriate age for your children to manage their inheritance.

There is no perfect solution on when to "hand over the reins" to a child.

Legacy

Creating or reviewing your estate plan offers peace of mind to you and your family members. And yet, there is another significant benefit. By following the principles of this book and living purposefully, you are opening yourself to transformation. When we enter into a personal relationship with Jesus, he doesn't transform one aspect of our lives. He transforms us completely. You'll be a healthier, happier version of yourself. Your familial relationships will improve.

If your time on earth is shorter than expected, do you want to pass down some of what you learned to the next generation? You may want to supplement estate documents with a family mission statement or letter. This statement could outline your values and express love for your children (living and unborn).

"Building and preserving family wealth isn't an end in itself," according to attorney Antoinette Bone[2]. "Rather, it's a tool for promoting shared family values—such as philanthropy, education, quality of life—or encouraging family members to lead responsible, productive, healthy lives. Drafting a family mission statement can be an effective way to define and communicate these values."

When you pass away, your family will obviously be devastated. Wouldn't it be wonderful to leave them a thoughtful message, sharing aspirations for children (and even grandchildren) for years to come?

Chapter Twelve

Cash Won't Pay for College

As parents, it's easy to think a college degree is a necessity. It is in our nature to want a better life for our kids. We often equate college with success.

However, with the rising costs of a college education, should we really consider a diploma the prerequisite for a satisfying career?

My oldest son is only nine years old, and I often envision him walking across the stage, standing proudly in a cap and gown as he receives his diploma. But what if the vision I have for him is not part of the plan for his life?

Meanwhile, my youngest son has learning difficulties, and it is too soon to tell if a traditional university degree is part of his future.

The ROI of College

Dr. Derek Tharp, a *Kitces.com* research associate, examined the value of investing in a college education[1]. Dr. Tharp recognized that there are two broad theories about why people invest in a college education. The first theory, the human capital model, contends that we go to college to build valuable skills and knowledge, which in turn enhances our productivity and enables us to earn more in the labor market. The second theory, the signaling model, suggests that college is simply a means for those with positive traits (e.g. intelligence, work ethic, and conformity) to demonstrate their capabilities to prospective employers in a credible way.

Economist Bryan Caplan's 2018 book, *The Case Against Education*[2], supports the signaling theory. He contends that the last semester of college is more heavily weighted than other semesters, and students wouldn't pursue "easy A's" if they were truly invested in acquiring new skills and knowledge. Caplan also explored the individual or private return on investment of college beyond the social aspect.

Academically speaking, students who achieve low grades have a far lower graduation rate than students with higher grades. Only 10 percent of those students obtain an undergraduate degree within four years, while 60 percent of top-performing students complete their bachelor's degree within the same time period. The return on investment is even worse for graduate degrees, with only 50 percent of excellent students finishing a master's degree in two years.

The bottom line is this: If your child is not performing well academically during high school, his or her college return on investment may be drastically lower than above-average students. Trade and vocational schools may be more suitable options.

What Does College Cost?

For those students who are interested and eager to attend college, start saving early! The cost of post-secondary education continues to outpace inflation, typically at a ratio of 2:1. According to *FinAid.org*[3], the historical average college tuition inflation rate was 8 percent, and tuition inflation rates recently hovered around 6 percent annually.

Cash won't entirely pay for college, even with financial aid (including scholarships, grants, and student loans).

If you intend to cover half the cost of college tuition at a four-year public university, multiply your child's age by $2,000 and aim to have at least that much set aside in college savings. Using this example, a 10-year-old should have $20,000 in a tax-advantaged account. Obviously, if you intend to send your child to a more expensive school or cover more than half the cost, the targeted amount should be even higher.

Some parents encourage their college-bound students to attend community college for two years and then transfer credits to a four-year university. The student later graduates with an undergraduate degree. This strategy often works for motivated students and saves money!

Competing Priorities

You probably have several competing saving priorities:
- Building emergency and opportunity funds
- Paying off debt
- Becoming financially independent
- Funding education expenses

Collectively, these goals feel daunting. First, focus on saving a few thousand dollars for true emergencies.

After the emergency fund, direct your attention to debt reduction. If you have high interest credit card debt, work on a plan to pay it off as quickly as possible. Accumulating an opportunity fund and saving for financial independence are important goals as well. At a minimum, if you work for an employer that offers a company-sponsored retirement plan, please take advantage of the free match.

Let's assume you have emergency and opportunity funds and your debt is under control. Additionally, you're saving for retirement through a 401(k) plan. Education savings should be your next priority.

Should You Save for Unborn Children?

Saving for unborn children may be a little extreme, especially if you have older children for whom you're already saving. If your older child does not use his or her 529 college savings plan, which is a tax-advantaged education account with minimal financial aid impact, you can change the beneficiary designation to a younger sibling.

Generally speaking, the earlier you save, the better. The 529 savings plans have aggressive age-based options where you can earn more in the early years of your child's life and potentially outpace college cost increases. You also have additional time to recover if the stock market crashes.

Make sure you are funding more than the minimum. Many 529 plans allow you to invest only $25 per month. That's just $300 a year. Even with tax deferral, saving $300 annually is unlikely to make a dent towards college expenses. I had a friend experience this firsthand. She started saving when her daughter was young but only the minimum amount. Her daughter had stellar grades and loads of extracurricular involvement in high school, but my friend and her husband simply could not afford to pay the "Expected Family Contribution" as determined by the financial aid officers. She wishes she set aside more money for college and regrets not having a trusted advisor to suggest a specific monthly savings goal.

How to Save

According to Fidelity's 2016 study[4], 72% of US families are saving for college, but only 41% have a 529 college savings account. In my professional opinion, 529 plans are the gold standard for college savings. There are no income restrictions for contributions. Assets grow tax deferred and can be withdrawn tax free for qualified higher education expenses.

Nonetheless, a 529 plan is not the only education savings plan that offers tax advantages. Savings bonds, Coverdell ESAs, and Roth IRAs are other alternatives.

Series EE and Series I saving bonds are backed by the federal government, but interest rates are historically low, and it may be more suitable to use another savings vehicle for college.

Coverdell Education Savings Accounts (ESA) were once very popular for private K through 12 expenses. However, with the Tax Cuts and Jobs Act of 2017, 529 savings plans now allow withdrawals of up to $10,000 per year per child for private elementary and high school expenses. Coverdell ESAs also have fallen in popularity due to stringent contribution rules.

You've likely heard of a Roth IRA as a retirement planning tool, and earnings in a Roth IRA grow tax free even though you don't receive a tax break on contributions. The maximum contribution is $5,500 annually for owners under age 50. For IRA owners aged 50 and older, an extra $1,000 "catch-up" contribution is allowed. Check the contribution limits, which are based on income, prior to contributing.

You always are able to withdraw the exact amount of Roth IRA contributions without penalty. However, withdrawing *earnings* could subject you to a 10 percent penalty if you do not meet one of the exceptions. **Qualified higher education expenses** for you, your spouse, children, and even grandchildren are one such exception.

Roth IRAs allow you to select the underlying investments for your account. This can be wonderful if you like to control the investment options and are well informed of the underlying risks and potential rewards. However, some people prefer just a few investment options, or they hire an advisor to assist with investment selection.

Of the three alternatives to 529 plans, I like Roth IRAs the best because they could be used for retirement if not used for higher education costs.

Two Types of 529 Plans

There are two primary types of 529 plans: *savings* and *prepaid*.

SAVINGS PLANS

The 529 college **savings** plans are the more common type of 529 plan. You establish the plan in the state of your choosing, either directly or through an advisor, and investments are selected that will *hopefully* increase over time.

Direct 529 savings plans are available for lower cost than their advisor-sold alternatives. Any investor who directly opens a 529 savings plan account should recognize that the account value will change. Aggressive investment values move as the stock market increases or decreases.

The 529 savings plan balances grow tax deferred and can be used for a plethora of higher education expenses, including tuition, fees, and room and board (for students enrolled at least half time). State income tax deductions may be offered for 529 savings plan contributions, but realize that deductions are **state-specific**.

PREPAID PLANS

Within a prepaid plan, you set aside money at today's tuition rates for a college that your child will attend later. Historically, prepaid plans were state run and offered advance tuition credits for in-state universities only.

What if your child plans to attend a private, rather than public, university? Private College 529 Plan[5] is the only prepaid 529 plan not run by a state, and the member college guarantees that your family purchases tomorrow's tuition at today's prices in the form of tuition certificates. Tuition can be used at any existing or future member private schools. Fortunately, the account owner need not pay any fee to establish or maintain the plan; all deposits are directly used to pay tuition.

One downside of prepaid plans is that the account balance can be applied only to tuition and mandatory fees—not room and board. Another potential downside happens when you contribute to a particular plan and your child does not select that college. For example, a former client funded a substantial Private College 529 plan but her daughter chose an in-state public university instead.

Market Risk

One major benefit of the prepaid, Private College 529 plan is that you avoid market risk. Let's say your son is five years away from attending college and you put $10,000 into the **prepaid plan** now. Suppose that covers 40 percent of first year tuition ($25K); it will still cover 40 percent of the first-year tuition at your son's private college in five years.

The same $10,000 contribution into a 529 college savings plan today could be worth $8,000 or $12,000 five years later. It is anyone's guess.

Tax Implications

Contributions to 529 plans are not limited by earnings. You could earn a million dollars this year and still contribute to a 529 plan. Gift tax rules apply, which means you can fund up to $15,000 per beneficiary in 2019 without any tax consequences. The term "beneficiary" refers to the person receiving the benefit—in this case, the future college student. If you have a sizable financial windfall and want to fund more than $15,000 per beneficiary, you can "superfund" the 529 plan and contribute $75,000 in 2019. Married couples can double that amount by "gift splitting" and filing separate gift tax returns.

Earlier, we talked about Coverdell ESAs as an alternative to 529 plans. Although you can use Coverdell money for college *OR* private K through 12 expenses, income limitations may prevent you from contributing to a Coverdell. The Tax Cuts and Jobs Act of 2017 allows you to withdraw up to $10,000 annually from a 529 plan on those expenses. That means you are not limited by a certain level of earnings. You can now save for college, private elementary, and high school expenses in a single account—the 529 plan.

Another added benefit of the 529 plan is that your beneficiary doesn't need to be a certain age. You could fund a 529 plan for yourself if you plan to incur higher education expenses. You also can change beneficiaries if you discover the original beneficiary no longer plans to attend college or receives a full-ride scholarship. Siblings, nieces, and nephews are great substitute beneficiaries.

Contributions to 529 plans grow tax deferred, and qualified distributions are tax free. Tax deferred means you are contributing "after-tax" money, and that contribution will grow without any immediate tax consequence. By definition, qualified 529 savings plan withdrawals include tuition, fees, books, equipment, and supplies. Room and board are considered "qualified" if the student is enrolled at least half time at a university or vocational school. You will not pay any income tax or penalty on 529 plan withdrawals if they are considered "qualified" education expenses.

For nonqualified withdrawals, you can remove your *contributions* tax free but will pay income tax and a 10 percent penalty on earnings. Let's assume you contributed $50,000 to a 529 plan that is now worth $75,000 and you want to withdraw the entire $75,000 for *non-college* expenses. You avoid paying tax on the $50,000 contribution. However, you will pay tax and a 10 percent penalty on $25,000 of earnings. If you spend the entire $75,000 balance on qualified expenses, you will not pay any income tax or penalty.

Financial Aid

When your child is ready to enter college, you need to complete a Free Application for Federal Student Aid, commonly known as FAFSA, to report your assets and income. The FAFSA application is a key part of the overall financial aid award. Even if your child is strictly looking for merit rather than need-based aid, many universities still require you to submit the FAFSA with your child's admission application.

Even if owned by the student, 529 plans count as parental assets on the FAFSA. This is actually a better result for most families. In the student's Expected Family Contribution calculation, parental assets are assessed at **5.64 percent**. Student assets, however, are assessed at **20 percent.** A higher Expected Family Contribution means a lower financial aid award. Any 529 plan withdrawal from a parent or student-owned 529 plan in one year is excluded from FAFSA's income calculation the next year.

This is a stark contrast to 529 plans owned by grandparents or other relatives. A grandparent should be very careful when she or he withdraws 529 plan assets for a grandchild. For financial aid, it is best to wait until a student's junior or senior year of college to withdraw money from a 529 plan owned by the grandparent. The 529 plan funds withdrawn in the freshman or sophomore year of college from a grandparent-owned 529 plan could later be counted as income.

Let's return to the FAFSA and Expected Family Contribution for a moment. The formula for computing EFC counts the following financial resources as being available to pay college expenses:
- 20 percent of a student's assets
- 50 percent of a student's income
- 2.6-5.6 percent of a parent's assets
- 22-47 percent of a parent's income, based on a sliding income scale and after certain allowances

Qualified retirement accounts like IRAs and 401(k) plans are excluded from the Expected Family Contributions computation. However, taking a withdrawal from a traditional or Roth IRA to pay for college could jeopardize financial aid the following year by counting it as income. Home equity, family-owned business equity, insurance policies, and annuities also are excluded from your assets when determining Expected Family Contributions on the FAFSA. The College Scholarship Service (CSS) Profile used by several private colleges has other rules, and they are too complex to go into detail here.

As you can see, there are many aspects of financial aid. The rules are constantly changing, so please diligently research this topic when your child is college-bound.

Are You Convinced?

Do you agree that a cash savings account is inadequate to fund most four-year degrees? It is not impossible but highly unlikely. Instead, consider tax-advantaged accounts like 529 plans or Roth IRAs as you plan for your children's future. *Savingforcollege.com*[6] is an excellent supplemental resource on college saving strategies, financial aid, and other technical topics covered in this chapter. Additionally, I will develop an online course on college planning through *redefiningfamilywealth.com*.

Chapter Thirteen

DIY is Good, but Advisors Are Better

If you read the previous chapters in this book, you have a much better understanding of personal finance than the typical American adult. But sometimes, that isn't enough. Generalities can only take you so far. You want more detailed information on how to reach your family's financial goals, and you need it tailored to your specific situation.

> "Plans fail for lack of counsel, but with many advisers they succeed."
>
> *– Proverbs 15:22*

I equate hiring a financial advisor with hiring a personal trainer. You may be able to join a gym or exercise regularly on your own. However, that may not get you to your goal.

You're making an additional monetary investment to get results! If you find yourself in a similar situation when it comes to financial goals, hiring a holistic financial planner could be your saving grace.

Not all financial advisors are created equal. In fact, there is huge variability in how advisors are compensated and the standards to which they are held. "Conflicted advice is costing America's working families about $17 billion per year in IRAs alone," according to a report from the President's Council of Economic Advisers. Now, for a history lesson.

Financial Services Industry - Past

Historically, when the financial services industry emerged, there were traditional "stockbrokers" who recommended investments to their clients. The broker (registered with a broker dealer firm) received a commission, and the client earned or lost money on the investment. Pretty straightforward, right? Essentially, most stockbrokers were salespeople. The more investment products they sold, the more money they had in their pocket.

The Industry - Present

Clients eventually wanted their broker's advice on other issues indirectly related to investments, such as retirement planning, debt reduction, and tax strategies. A new wave of financial advisory companies emerged to meet this demand: Registered Investment Advisory firms, or RIAs.

A financial advisor will generally fall in one of three camps:
- Fee-based broker

- Fee-only RIA
- A hybrid, meaning the advisor can work under the brokerage or RIA

Let's talk about the fiduciary standard and what it means for you, especially when seeking a financial advisor. When a professional is acting in your best interest, she is following the *fiduciary standard*. The *suitability standard* held by many traditional brokers is more lenient.

An Illustration

Suppose you walk into Ann Taylor to buy a dress for an upcoming social event. You see one that catches your eye and proceed to the fitting room. As you glance at yourself in the mirror, you notice that the color makes you look a little pale and doesn't look great around your midsection. But you're shopping alone and know that fitting room mirrors can be deceiving. You step outside and ask the fitting room clerk for a second opinion, "How does this dress look on me?"

If the fitting room clerk is operating under a suitability standard, she may say something like, "It looks nice. I think you should buy it."

If instead the fitting room clerk is held to the higher fiduciary standard, she can recommend only a dress that looks fantastic on you (it's in your best interest). The fiduciary clerk may respond, "Hmmm. I like this dress on you but think this other one may look even better." You try on the new dress and love it. The color is perfect, and it fits wonderfully.

The fitting room clerk doesn't earn a commission. Under either standard, she doesn't have a financial incentive to recommend one dress over another. Yet if held to the fiduciary standard, her recommendation *must be in your best interest*.

One More Thing

Let's take the same example one step further. Suppose you are still shopping for a dress but go into a store where the associates are paid on commission. You look at two dresses—one priced at $100 and the other at $150. Both dresses look good on you, but this commission-based sales associate will get a larger check if she recommends the more expensive dress. When you ask her opinion, she suggests the $150 dress.

Regrettably, you could walk into a financial advisor's office today and not know if that advisor is operating under a fiduciary standard or suitability standard unless you directly ask him or conduct online research in advance. In 2017, US legislators unfortunately vetoed a law that would have increased transparency, making it easier for prospective clients to know if an advisor is operating under the less-stringent suitability standard.

In October 2019, the rules will change with a new Code of Ethics and Standards of Conduct. This industry standard means all Certified Financial Planner™ (CFP®) professionals will be required to act as fiduciaries in their clients' best interest at all times. If advisors don't follow the standards, they could lose their license. This change is a great win for consumers.

Compensation

Bottom line: If you want to work with a financial advisor, look for a Certified Financial Planner™. Even better, find one who is "fee only" and doesn't work on commission. The National Association of Personal Financial Advisors (NAPFA) is the leading association of fee-only professionals[1] whose only source of compensation comes directly from you, the client. In other words, advice and compensation are totally independent of product recommendations.

Fee-based advisors *sound* a lot like fee-only advisors but actually operate differently. Fee-based advisors can accept fees for their guidance and investment oversight but *also* can receive commissions on specific investment products (e.g. annuities, life insurance policies, loaded mutual funds, etc.). This could create a conflict of interest for the fee-based advisor. If he has the choice between selling an annuity and earning a more substantial commission than one on a passive exchange-traded fund, he may suggest the annuity.

It All Boils Down to Trust

Trust is critical, and a 2016 poll by the American Association of Individual Investors proves it. About 65% of respondents said they mistrust the financial services industry; only 2% of respondents trust financial professionals "a lot." That means 98% of the US population doesn't place a lot of trust in his or her financial advisor. How sad! Consumers benefit when advisors break away from conflicted fee-based environments.

Questions to Ask an Advisor

Now that you have some background on the types of advisors and their standards, let's turn to the kinds of questions you may want to ask when selecting a financial advisor. The exact list of questions is subjective, and my list below comes from several different sources[2]. Obviously, you may not have time to ask all of these questions during an initial consultation. Instead, try to gather as much data as you can in advance by reviewing a firm's website and the LinkedIn profiles of its advisors.

1. Are you held to a fiduciary standard at all times?
2. How are you compensated?
3. Who is your ideal client? Do you have other clients like me?
4. How long have you been practicing? Please tell me more about your experience and qualifications.
5. Have you ever been publicly disciplined for unethical actions?
6. What happens to my relationship with the firm if something happens to you?
7. What is your investment philosophy?
8. How will you help me reach my financial goals?
9. What assumptions do you use for retirement planning illustrations?
10. Can you explain the concept of active versus passive investing to me?
11. Do you own the same investment products you'll recommend to me?
12. How did you handle the 2008 downturn?
13. How do you invest in yourself?
14. Why did you choose this work?
15. How do you use technology for my benefit?

Additionally, you want to hire an advisor who can clearly articulate financial concepts in a way you understand them. Other examples of concept-oriented questions like #10 include:

a. How do you determine how much money should be in stocks versus bonds?

b. What do you think of annuities?

Don't be discouraged if the first few advisors you interview aren't a good fit. Finding an advisor who is attuned to your needs takes time. It's like dating. You may have to go on a couple of bad first dates before you find the love of your life.

If you've asked at least a couple of questions and are satisfied with the advisor's initial answers, dig deeper. Questions at this stage should focus on communication. How often will you be meeting with the advisor? In person or virtually? How quickly will that advisor respond to email or phone calls? Are you going to work initially with this advisor, only to be "handed off" to a less experienced firm associate as time goes on?

Again, it comes down to fit. If you are a Type A personality who wants a returned phone call within an hour of leaving the message, you may not work well with an advisor who returns calls within two business days. If you live an hour away from the advisor's office and really value in-person meetings, find out if that advisor is willing to come to you or meet at a central location. Technology enthusiasts who prefer to hop on a virtual video conference will find it easy to work with an advisor who is hundreds or thousands of miles away. Know yourself and the expectations you have for the working relationship.

If married, make sure that your spouse likes the advisor, too. The American College State Farm Center for Women and Financial Services[3] examined the extent to which widows leave their financial advisors after a spouse's death. Of those surveyed, 46% of widows left the advisor. Approximately 39% of widows who left felt they didn't have a good relationship with their advisor, and 36% felt their advisor was unhelpful or didn't understand them.

Husbands: if you die before your wife, do you really want her to end the advisory relationship at a time she is most vulnerable and needs assistance?

Wives: even if you let your husband take the lead on financial matters, you also are responsible for the financial health of your household. Voice any concerns you have about the financial advisor.

Spouses should be equal participants in the financial planning process, and an advisor should have that same mantra. Proceed with caution if the advisor is aware you are happily married and is perfectly fine working with only one of you. He or she should be looking at your joint financial goals. Call me old school, but I'm of the opinion that "two shall become one" when they celebrate the sacrament of matrimony.

In fact, I had a prospective client contact me by phone on a Friday afternoon. He and I had a great conversation, and he wanted to start working with me. I was really excited and thought this advisory relationship would be wonderful, but I said, "Wait. I know you're married and haven't spoken to your wife yet. She doesn't know anything about me. Please let's schedule a time to talk with her, too, so I can ensure this will be a good working relationship for both of you." He agreed, and she was part of the formal introductory meeting.

Hourly Arrangements

Much of the focus of this chapter is finding and vetting a financial advisor with whom you will have a long-term relationship. However, there may be a time in your life where an hourly arrangement may be more appropriate.

Deciding between a one-time, hourly engagement or ongoing relationship with a financial advisor can be difficult. Look to what you are trying to accomplish.

Do you have a single, urgent need that must be addressed? Can you afford to work with an advisor on an ongoing basis? Hourly advice may be sufficient.

If you have concerns in multiple areas such as cash flow, insurance, tax mitigation, investments, and debt, it may be better to work with a financial professional on a long-term basis who can walk with you as new challenges and questions arise.

Tread Carefully as a DIYer

Doing it yourself is tempting. When faced with a home renovation project, Bryan and I roll up our sleeves and do most of the work ourselves. However, we know our limitations. We aren't experienced plumbers or electricians. If we're finishing the basement, we are going to hire professionals for the bathroom and lighting installation.

Similarly, you should recognize your limitations. Do you have any training in personal financial planning and investment management? If not, are you willing to invest time and money into learning how to manage financial assets and stay accountable to your goals?

Think about one thing you hope to accomplish within the next 365 days. Now fast forward a year. Did you achieve the goal? Did you have a trusted advisor standing alongside you, or were you able to do it on your own?

Chapter Fourteen

Ready, Set, Go

What does purposeful living mean to you? Have you ever taken the time to really think about it? Our lives are busy and filled with commitments: Work. Appointments. Kids' activities. The list could go on and on. Each day, we have 86,400 seconds to further our goals. That's 1,440 minutes, or 24 hours. Are you using that precious time to pursue your dreams?

How Do You Define Success?

Each person's definition of success is unique. For you, what does success look like? Is it a deeper faith relationship? Better marriage? Stronger relationship with kids? Physical health? Greater satisfaction at work?

Don't limit yourself to being successful in a single area. I like to blend them. For me, purposeful living (and success) means:

1. Having faith in God, surrendering to His plan, and trusting Him completely.

2. Cultivating a stronger marriage with Bryan, acting as his cheerleader.
3. Being an exemplary mother, choosing compassion even in chaotic moments.
4. Serving others using my unique talents and gifts.

Integration of Vision, Values, and Goals
Vision → Values → Goals

Articulating a vision takes time and patience. Don't rush it. Psychologist Angela Duckworth says the secret to outstanding achievement isn't talent. Rather, it is a blend of persistence and passion also known as grit[1].

Once you have a clear vision, it is essential to reflect on your values. Not only your individual values but also the ones you have as a family. Visit *redefiningfamilywealth.com* for additional resources on vision and values. Understand that values are different from goals. Values have not been imposed on you. You choose them after careful reflection. They are guiding principles that define your daily interactions.

Susan David's book, *Emotional Agility*, cites the following characteristics of values:
- Freely chosen
- Ongoing, not fixed
- Active
- Bring freedom from social comparisons

Before bedtime each night, I mentally run through the day. When were my actions aligned with my values? When weren't they aligned? What can I do differently tomorrow to become a better version of myself? Monitoring goals doesn't happen as regularly for me, but I'm consistently able to assess whether my actions reflect deeply-held values.

SMART Goals

Once you've articulated a broad vision and defined your core values, you're ready to move on to the next step: Goal creation. SMART is a helpful acronym for goal setting. *Mindtools.com*[2] relies on Peter Drucker's Management by Objectives concepts to define the acronym:
- **S**pecific
- **M**easurable
- **A**chievable
- **R**elevant
- **T**ime Bound

Following the SMART framework may be powerful but it is missing two key ingredients: Excitement and risk. Continuously operating within your comfort zone causes stagnancy. Michael Hyatt's book, *Your Best Year Ever*, articulates a detailed plan for achieving your most important goals. Hyatt builds on the SMART acronym and developed the SMARTER framework:

- **S**pecific
- **M**easurable
- **A**ctionable
- **R**isky
- **T**ime-Keyed
- **E**xciting
- **R**elevant

You get the idea. When you start with an overarching vision and identify values that support it, individual goals help you live out that vision. Regardless of how you define goal setting, recognize that there is a time component. Visions rarely have an end date, whereas achievement goals always have an endpoint. Habit goals are ongoing activities used to support achievement goals. Hyatt firmly believes you improve your odds of success when you make a goal relevant to your stage of life, personal values, and other goals.

For example, if Aaron and his wife, Sue, both work outside the home full time and have four young kids, Aaron is unlikely to accomplish a goal of completing the Ironman. It's a very difficult goal to achieve during this season of life.

But if Dave were single with no kids, setting a goal to complete the Ironman by the end of the year would certainly be achievable. In that case, Dave's habit goal might be a one-hour workout six days per week until the race was complete.

Here's another example: Suppose you set a goal to pay down $12,000 of debt in a year. One of your other goals is to strengthen your marriage and go on 12 dates with your spouse over the same 12-month period. The first goal contradicts the second goal. You need to allocate $1,000 a month toward debt repayment but you're still spending money to go out frequently for extravagant dates. You are setting yourself up for failure!

Consider reducing each of the goals; aim to pay down $6,000 of debt and change the date-night frequency to every other month for the next 12 months. Or plan "free" dates at home. By making the goal more realistic, perhaps you **can** afford to do both.

Divine Intervention

Sometimes, we can hold too tightly to our vision and forget about God's purpose for us. Clearly identified goals may be knocked off course. In the moment, we see it as a disruption.

But after the dust clears and things are put into perspective, you may realize God had to take the steering wheel because you were drifting off course.

> God wants to reorder our priorities. He wants to transform us. Many times, this means we need to step outside our comfort zones. If we sincerely and truly trust in the Lord, we cannot solely depend on our human understanding.

In January 2017, I set an ambitious goal to launch the first online course for WorthyNest® within six months. I made progress, but my 65-year-old mother had some unexpected medical issues. She was in and out of hospital, and I was by her side. Through God's grace and saving power, she miraculously healed and began the recovery process.

I turned my attention back to my business and eventually got to where I wanted to be. I was behind in my original goal, but was it really missing the mark if God had another plan? I don't think so. The days spent in the hospital with my mother were a gift. Full of love and hope. They weren't taken for granted.

Are You Ready?

Are you ready to follow the plan destined for you? Are you willing to live purposefully and intentionally? Do you have specific, short-term goals to support that vision? You and your family are worthy of a brighter future. Now go make it happen!

Acknowledgments

My heartfelt thanks extend to so many people. First, to my family. Bryan, you are my rock. Thank you for being my biggest cheerleader throughout this writing journey. Boys, I love you more than you could know and hope the lessons in this book will be valuable when you eventually experience the joy of adulthood. Mom and Dad, thanks for the values you instilled in me as a young girl and the guidance you continue to provide. To my older sister, Julie, thank you for your unending support and book edit recommendations. We may not see each other as much as we may like but I know you're only a phone call or email away.

Additional thanks to:

Julie Broad and the entire team at Book Launchers for taking a manuscript and turning it into a published book. I appreciate the content and copy edits, design services, and marketing support you so generously provided.

Jeff Goins for giving me the confidence to call myself a writer. At your Tribe conference in 2017, God placed it on my heart to write this book. I also really appreciate the one-on-one outline coaching you provided in the summer of 2018.

My current and former clients, for whom I am grateful. Without you, I wouldn't have real-life examples to share. You challenge me to become a better person every day.

XY Planning Network and FinCon community members, for your excitement and enthusiasm for personal finance. It's great to be part of two growing communities who consistently think outside the box.

To all the other writers whose work has inspired or encouraged me.

Finally, and most importantly, I thank God for His unending grace. You gave me the words to write this book and the courage to publish it.

Notes

Chapter 1: You Were Made for More

1. Institute for Faith, Work, and Economics, "Four Principles of Biblical Stewardship" https://tifwe.org/four-principles-of-biblical-stewardship/

2. Matthew Kelly, *The Biggest Lie in the History of Christianity*

    https://dynamiccatholic.com/the-biggest-lie-in-the-history-of-christianity-hardcover

3. Michael Kitces' *Financial Advisor Success* podcast

    https://www.kitces.com/blog/diane-macphee-dmac-consulting-services-podcast-financial-advisor-coach-pcc/

4. Lisa Eadiciccio, *Time*, "Americans Check Their Phones 8 Billion Times a Day" http://time.com/4147614/smartphone-usage-us-2015/

5. Alli Worthington, *Fierce Faith: A Woman's Guide to Fighting Fear, Wrestling Worry, and Overcoming Anxiety*

    https://www.amazon.com/Fierce-Faith-Fighting-Wrestling-Overcoming/dp/0310342252

6. Daniel Tencer, *The Huffington Post*, "85% of Jobs That Will Exist in 2030 Haven't Been Invented Yet: Dell"

    https://www.huffingtonpost.ca/2017/07/14/85-of-jobs-that-will-exist-in-2030-haven-t-been-invented-yet-d_a_23030098/

Chapter 2: Your Past Isn't a Script for Your Future

1. Steven Covey, *Seven Habits of Highly Effective People*

    https://www.franklincovey.com/the-7-habits.html

2. Nicolette Stinson, *Chopra.com*, "10 Steps to Develop an Abundance Mindset" https://chopra.com/articles/10-steps-to-develop-an-abundance-mindset

3. Our World in Data

https://ourworldindata.org/a-history-of-global-living-conditions-in-5-charts

4. Jon Acuff, *Finish*

https://acuff.me/books/

5. Dr. Thomas Stanley, *The Millionaire Next Door*

http://www.thomasjstanley.com/publication/the-millionaire-next-door/

6. Dr. Thomas Stanley and Dr. Sarah Stanley Fallaw, *The Next Millionaire Next Door*

https://www.amazon.com/Next-Millionaire-Door-Enduring-Strategies-ebook/dp/B07G5HHFW6?

7. Dr. Carol Dweck, *Mindset: The New Psychology of Success* https://www.amazon.com/Mindset-Psychology-Carol-S-Dweck/dp/0345472322

8. Keith Payne and Pascal Sheeran, *Behavioral Scientist,* "Try to Resist Misinterpreting the Marshmallow Test" http://behavioralscientist.org/try-to-resist-misinterpreting-the-marshmallow-test/

Chapter 3: Lead with Values

1. Joshua Becker, *Simple Money*, "Your Biggest Expense is Your Greatest Opportunity" (Issue 1, October 2018)

2. Janet Porteman, *Lawyers.com*, "Petty Theft and Shoplifting"

https://www.lawyers.com/legal-info/criminal/criminal-law-basics/shoplifting-or-petty-theft-whats-the-big-deal.html

3. Ron Leiber, *The Opposite of Spoiled*

https://www.amazon.com/Opposite-Spoiled-Raising-Grounded-Generous-ebook/dp/B00KAC65PW

4. Share Save Spend®

http://www.sharesavespend.com

5. FamZoo

http://famzoo.com/

6. ProActive

Notes

https://proactivebudget.com/

7. Stockpile

https://www.stockpile.com

8. Worthy

https://joinworthy.com/

Chapter 5: Prepare for Opportunities, Not Just Emergencies

1. Maslow's Hierarchy of Needs diagram from researchgate.net

2. Covey, *Seven Habits of Highly Effective People*

https://www.franklincovey.com/the-7-habits.html

3. Gallup, "State of the American Workforce" Feb 2017 Report https://news.gallup.com/reports/178514/state-american-workplace.aspx

4. Jon Acuff, *Finish*

https://acuff.me/books/

5. Michael Hyatt, *Your Best Year Ever*

https://yourbestyeareverbook.com

Chapter 6: Not All Debt is Evil

1. Simple Tuition by Lending Tree, https://www.simpletuition.com/student-loans/federal/

2. Student Aid, https://studentaid.ed.gov/sa/types/loans/subsidized-unsubsidized#how-much

3. PR Newswire "Average New Car Prices Jump 2% for March 2018" https://www.prnewswire.com/news-releases/average-new-car-prices-jump-2-percent-for-march-2018-on-suv-sales-strength-according-to-kelley-blue-book-300623110.html

4. Brett Oblack, "Step 1 Minimalist," guest post on Joshua Becker's Becoming Minimalist site under "5 Ways Minimalism Can Help Create a Stronger Marriage" https://www.becomingminimalist.com/5-ways-minimalism-can-help-create-a-stronger-marriage/

Chapter 7: Values-Based Investing Works

1. CNBC, "Bad Times for Active Managers" https://www.cnbc.com/2017/04/12/bad-times-for-active-managers-almost-none-have-beaten-the-market-over-the-past-15-years.html

Chapter 8: Even the Faithful Have Insurance (but You Can't Emergency Proof Your Life)

1. TMA Insurance Trust: 10 Important Statistics in Honor of Disability Insurance Awareness Month

    https://www.tmait.org/blog/10-important-statistics-in-honor-of-disability-insurance-awareness-month

2. Jonathan Cohn, *The Huffington Post*, "There's a Christian Alternative to Obamacare. But There's a Catch." (March 9, 2018)

    https://www.huffingtonpost.com/entry/christian-health-ministry-obamacare_us_5a9d66fee4b0a0ba4ad6754b

3. Take Command Health

    https://www.takecommandhealth.com

Chapter 9: Traditional Retirement Isn't the Answer

1. *Actforlibraries.org* "How Medical Technology is Improving Our Life Span" http://www.actforlibraries.org/how-medical-technology-is-improving-our-life-span/

2. Grace Donnelly, *Fortune*, "Life Expectancy: Why It Dropped in the U.S. This Year" http://fortune.com/2018/02/09/us-life-expectancy-dropped-again/

3. Amy Morin, *verywellmind.com*, "Depression Statistics Everyone Should Know" https://www.verywellmind.com/depression-statistics-everyone-should-know-4159056

4. Mitch Anthony, *The New Retirementality*

    https://www.amazon.com/New-Retirementality-Planning-Living-Dreams/dp/1118705122/ref=sr_1_1?s=books&ie=UTF8&qid=1529586751&sr=1-1&keywords=the+new+retirementality

5. What Are B Corps? http://www.bcorporation.net/what-are-b-corps

Notes

6. *KitDarby.com,* Aviation Consulting tweet

https://twitter.com/KitDarby/status/953099425345359873/photo/1?ref_src=twsrc%5Etfw&ref_url=http%3A%2F%2Fkitdarby.com%2Fwp%2Fcareer-development%2F

Chapter 10: Go for Broke

1. *IRS Publication 526*

https://www.irs.gov/pub/irs-pdf/p526.pdf

2. *Charity Navigator*

https://www.charitynavigator.org

3. *Good Meets World*

https://www.goodmeetsworld.com

4. National Philanthropic Trust "What Is a Donor-Advised Fund (DAF)?" https://www.nptrust.org/what-is-a-donor-advised-fund/

5. *Giving Tuesday* https://www.givingtuesday.org

6. Katie Rogers, *The New York Times,* "The Ice Bucket Challenge Helped Scientists Discover a New Gene Tied to A.L.S."

https://www.nytimes.com/2016/07/28/health/the-ice-bucket-challenge-helped-scientists-discover-a-new-gene-tied-to-als.html

7. Micah Bales, *Red Letter Christians,* "Give It All Away: Could Jesus Possibly Have Meant What He Said About Money?"

https://www.redletterchristians.org/give-it-all-away-could-jesus-possibly-have-meant-what-he-said-about-money/

Chapter 11: Get Your Affairs in Order (You'll Thank Me Later)

1. *Kirk Estate Planning* blog

https://kirkestateplanning.blogspot.com/2018/03/8-good-reasons-to-create-your-will-or.html

2. *The Law Offices of Antoinette Bone* blog

https://abonelaw.com/family-mission-statement/

Chapter 12: Cash Won't Pay for College

1. Dr. Derek Tharp, *Kitces.com,* "Why the Best ROI on College May Be for Those Who Would Have Been Successful Anyway"

https://www.kitces.com/blog/benefits-of-attending-college-signaling-theory-bryan-caplan-case-against-education/

2. Bryan Caplan, *The Case Against Education*

https://www.amazon.com/Case-against-Education-System-Waste/dp/0691174652/ref=as_li_ss_tl?ie=UTF8&qid=1519610764&sr=8-1&keywords=case+against+education&&linkCode=sl1&tag=kitcescom-20&linkId=443860704e32cb76ae1ec2a9c3e00f0d

3. Tuition Inflation http://www.finaid.org/savings/tuition-inflation.phtml

4. Fidelity's 10-Year College Progress Report

https://www.fidelity.com/about-fidelity/individual-investing/10-year-college-progress-report

5. Private College 529 Plan https://www.privatecollege529.com/OFI529/theme/pc529/learn-more/plan-details.jsp

6. Saving for College

https://www.savingforcollege.com/college_savings_201

Chapter 13: DIY is Good, but Advisors Are Better

1. The National Association of Personal Financial Advisors, "About Us" https://www.napfa.org/about-us

2. Sources for questions to ask a financial advisor include:

   a. Dana Anspach, *The Balance*, "Questions to Ask a Potential Financial Advisor" (updated August 13, 2017) https://www.thebalance.com/questions-to-potential-financial-advisor-2388445 -

   b. CFP Board, *Let's Make a Plan*, "How to Choose a Financial Advisor" http://www.letsmakeaplan.org/other-resources/selecting-an-advisor

   c. National Association of Personal Financial Advisors (NAPFA), "How to Find Your Financial Advisor" https://www.napfa.org/financial-planning/how-to-find-an-advisor

   d. Lou Carlozo, *US News & World Report*, "20 Questions to Ask Before Hiring a Financial Advisor, US News & World Report (April 8, 2015) https://money.usnews.com/money/personal-finance/mutual-funds/articles/2015/04/08/20-questions-to-ask-before-hiring-a-financial-advisor

3. The American College of Financial Services, "Statistics Financial Advisors Should Understand About Working with Widows"

https://womenscenter.theamericancollege.edu/sites/womenscenter/files/Statistics_Financial_Advisors_Should_Understand.pdf -

Chapter 14: Ready, Set, Go

1. Lisa Quest, *Forbes*, "Why Grit is More Important Than IQ When You're Trying to Become Successful" (March 6, 2017)

https://www.forbes.com/sites/lisaquast/2017/03/06/why-grit-is-more-important-than-iq-when-youre-trying-to-become-successful/#11929fbd7e45

2. *MindTools*, "SMART Goals: How to Make Your Goals Achievable"

https://www.mindtools.com/pages/article/smart-goals.htm

CPSIA information can be obtained
at www.ICGtesting.com
Printed in the USA
BVHW032012010320
573677BV00005B/9